SpringerBriefs in Finance

SpringerBriefs present concise summaries of cutting-edge research and practical applications across a wide spectrum of fields. Featuring compact volumes of 50 to 125 pages, the series covers a range of content from professional to academic. Typical topics might include: a timely report of state-of-the art analytical techniques, a bridge between new research results, as published in journal articles, and a contextual literature review, a snapshot of a hot or emerging topic, an in-depth case study or clinical example, and a presentation of core concepts that students must understand in order to make independent contributions. SpringerBriefs in Finance showcase emerging theory, empirical research, and practical application in corporate finance, banking, financial management, behavioral finance, financial markets, social and entrepreneurial finance, microfinance, and related fields, from a global author community. Briefs are characterized by fast, global electronic dissemination, standard publishing contracts, standardized manuscript preparation and formatting guidelines, and expedited production schedules.

Elena Schmid • Michael Truebestein •
Matthias Daniel Aepli

Tokenization in Real Estate

Opportunities and Challenges

Springer

Elena Schmid
Jones Lang LaSalle AG
Zurich, Switzerland

Michael Truebestein
University of Lucerne
Rotkreuz, Switzerland

Matthias Daniel Aepli
University of Lucerne
Rotkreuz, Switzerland

ISSN 2193-1720 ISSN 2193-1739 (electronic)
SpringerBriefs in Finance
ISBN 978-3-031-55809-2 ISBN 978-3-031-55810-8 (eBook)
https://doi.org/10.1007/978-3-031-55810-8

This Springer imprint is published by the registered company Springer Nature Switzerland AG
The registered company address is: Gewerbestrasse 11, 6330 Cham, Switzerland

Management Summary

This book is an inductive exploratory study on the still novel topic of tokenization in real estate. Tokenization in real estate can refer to both the digital representation of a real estate asset and the digital representation of ownership of a real estate asset, often in combination with fractionalization. It is enabled through blockchain technology. This research aims to understand the concept, underlying technologies, opportunities, and challenges of tokenization in real estate.

Real estate is traditionally considered to be illiquid, difficult to access, lacking in transparency, time-consuming, and costly in its transaction and investment processes and has large capital requirements. Tokenization promises to overcome many of these common shortcomings. Its main advantages include increased liquidity, creating new sources of capital, and democratizing the asset class as entry barriers are lowered. Furthermore, decentralization, data transparency, and security are associated with the implementation of blockchain technology, while smart contracts can facilitate the automation of tasks.

In practice, there are a series of challenges hindering the full realization of these benefits. The Swiss regulatory framework does currently not allow for the direct tokenization and fractionalization of a real estate asset. Issuers must instead establish an intermediate structure to hold the asset, which can then be tokenized and fractionalized. This tears at the described benefits and might not be in line with the proposed notion of a decentralized real estate investment opportunity. A further aspect limiting development is the potential lack of demand for the resulting investment opportunities. It is unclear whether this stems from the novelty of the concept resulting in a lack of understanding and therefore trust, whether the missing secondary market exchange is causing hesitation or whether there truly is limited demand for tokenized and fractionalized real estate investment opportunities.

As part of this paper, three case studies were carried out on the three use cases of successfully tokenized real estate assets which can currently be found in Switzerland. This primary research demonstrated how tokenization in real estate differs from its theoretical exemplary idea. It, furthermore, illustrated how there are a variety of ways to set up the tokenization of a real estate asset, both from a technical and from a structural and legal perspective. Hereby, the analysis did not reveal one best practice to follow. The case studies were complemented with expert interviews. The interviewees reinforced many of the results of the secondary research. They further described how they entered the real estate token market early on, highlighting past and current challenges. All in all, they were confident that their achievements sent a strong message to the market and concluded that it is not a question of if a broader implementation of blockchain and tokenization will be seen but when.

Overall, the future role and scope of blockchain technology and tokenization are not yet clear. They might simply represent a new technological basis for the market to work on or they might shape the market to a larger extent. A wider implementation will require overcoming a series of challenges, however, the potential that blockchain and tokenization hold is significant. Also, markets and regulations are evolving favourably, and participants are convinced of the future of the concept. So, while blockchain and tokenization might not be the solution to all problems they are likely here to stay. To guide a wider adoption where the theoretical benefits can be realized as fully as possible, specific recommendations were formed as a result of this study. Hereby, five recommendations for the overall market environment and five recommendations to participants active within this market are suggested.

Keywords Real estate · Tokenization · Fractionalization · Blockchain

Contents

List of Abbreviations

AI	Artificial Intelligence
AML	Anti-Money Laundering
AMLA	Anti-Money Laundering Act (CH)
API	Application Programming Interface
B52	Bahnhofstrasse 52
BMT	BrickMark Token
CBDC	Central Bank Digital Currency
CFT	Combating the Financing of Terrorism
CRE	Commercial Real Estate
CSSF	Commission de Surveillance du Secteur Financier (Luxembourg)
DAC	Decentralized Autonomous Corporation
DAO	Decentralized Autonomous Organization
dApps	Decentralized Applications
DAS	Decentralized Autonomous Space
DLT	Distributed Ledger Technology
DPO	Digital Product Offering
DPoS	Delegated Proof-of-Stake
EIB	European Investment Bank
EO	Executive Order
EPRA	European Public Real Estate Association
ETH	Ether
FCA	Financial Conduct Authority (UK)
FINMA	Financial Market Supervisory Authority (CH)
FMA	Financial Market Authority (Liechtenstein)
ICO	Initial Coin Offering
IoT	Internet of Things
IPO	Initial Public Offering
KIID	Key Investor Information Document
KYC	Know your Customer
MAS	Monetary Authority of Singapore
MiCA	Markets in Crypto-Assets (EU)

NFT	Non-Fungible Token
ODX	Osaka Digital Exchange
OTC	Over-the-Counter
PBFT	Practical Byzantine Fault Tolerance
PoS	Proof-of-Stake
PoW	Proof-of-Work
REIT	Real Estate Investment Trust
ROM	Register of Members
SDX	SIX Digital Exchange
SEC	Securities and Exchange Commission (US)
SPV	Special Purpose Vehicle
TVTG	Tokens and Trustworthy Technologies Law (Liechtenstein)
VARA	Virtual Assets Regulatory Authority (Dubai)
XCHF	CryptoFranc

List of Figures

Chapter 1
Introduction

Real estate is considered one of the world's largest asset classes, valued at around $200 trillion. An unimaginably high sum. However, only around $19 trillion is currently accessible to investors through shares, funds, or other investment vehicles. The remaining properties, and resulting income, are in private or institutional ownership (Rind, 2021a, p. 94). The traditional real estate (investment) market is, furthermore, known for its illiquidity, high capital requirements, and complex and slow transaction processes. Tokenization and the application of blockchain technology promise to overcome many of these shortcomings (Smith et al., 2019, pp. 14, 26; Pang et al., 2020, p. 6). As a result, the concept of tokenization has received a lot of attention in recent years (Fonnesbæk Lodahl, 2021). However, existent academic research on the topic is still scarce.

Tokenization in real estate can refer to both the digital representation of a real estate asset and the digital representation of ownership of a real estate asset. Tokenization often also implies the fractionalization of said ownership rights. Both are enabled through the application of blockchain technology and usually also smart contracts. Both offer a series of advantages. The broad implementation of either, however, is difficult as the market is still in its early stages. Currently, further development is often limited as there are significant challenges to overcome, first and foremost, regulatory challenges (Smith et al., 2019, p. 7; Baum, 2020, p. 3). In Switzerland, however, the recent coming into force of the DLT Act has positively shaped the legal foundation (The Federal Council, 2021). Furthermore, the necessary underlying technology is available. So, with the legal and technical requirements met, the question of what a wider adoption of tokenization in real estate could look like remains. How can a wider adoption be achieved and what makes sense going forward?

In trying to answer these questions, an inductive exploratory study on the topic has been conducted. The research includes case studies on the three use cases of successfully tokenized real estate assets in Switzerland, intending to identify best

E. Schmid et al., *Tokenization in Real Estate*, SpringerBriefs in Finance,
https://doi.org/10.1007/978-3-031-55810-8_1

practices and lessons learnt. In addition, expert interviews were carried out to gain an in-depth understanding of the cases as well as gather more information on the regulatory situation in Switzerland. Coupled with a thorough literature review as well as research on the most recent developments in the real estate token market, a sound basis for analysis was established. Guided by the research questions, a conclusion was formed, and as a result, specific recommendations could be defined. These recommendations are specifically formulated for the situation in Switzerland and focus, on the one hand, on creating the optimal market environment suitable for a wider adoption and, on the other hand, on the actions recommended to different market participants.

Following this introduction, the objectives and specific research questions are presented. The paper then continues with a literature review and technical explanations of the underlying technologies. Having established this base, the focus shifts to tokenization in real estate. Again, a literature review is provided first, followed by the potential opportunities and challenges. Separate subchapters, furthermore, focus on the regulatory framework currently present in Switzerland and recent developments in the market, including a global perspective. Next, the methodology is presented. The primary research, three case studies, and expert interviews on use cases in Switzerland are then discussed. Finally, a conclusion and specific market recommendations are given.

1.1 Objectives and Research Questions

While tokenization in real estate is a trending topic in the industry, academic research is still limited and additional work is necessary. This paper seeks to establish an overview of the concept of tokenization, including its opportunities and challenges, to determine how a wider implementation could be achieved and what a wider implementation should look like. This includes reviewing the underlying technologies: distributed ledger technology, blockchain technology, smart contracts, and tokenization. It also includes a review of the developments and applications of tokenization in real estate so far. Here, concrete case studies on the tokenized real estate assets in Switzerland as well as expert interviews come into play. Finally, analysing all acquired data allows for a conclusion and specific recommendations for the Swiss market to be formed. Overall, the objective is to further strengthen the understanding and, as a result, the development of tokenization in real estate.

Due to the nature of the topic, which is still new to both the real estate market and the academic sphere, this paper follows an inductive exploratory research design. As a result, the following research questions are formulated broadly:

RQ1: What is tokenization in real estate and how does it work? What are the underlying technologies? RQ2: What does the implementation of tokenization look like, opportunities and challenges?

RQ3: Case studies and expert interviews: What are the current best practices and lessons learnt?

RQ4: What recommendations can be given to different market participants going forward?

1.1.1 Limitations

Naturally, the following research comes with a set of limitations. The most prominent being the novelty of the topic. Real estate tokenization is mostly discussed and researched theoretically. This means that there are only a few use cases to be reviewed. Additionally, current market situations, especially also the regulatory frameworks, differ strongly between countries. These variations between countries make it difficult for global recommendations to be formed. As a result, a focus is set on the Swiss market.

Furthermore, tokenization in real estate is developing quickly. The market is continuously evolving, and participants are experimenting with its application. Consequently, new information is frequently hitting the market. This in turn means that the conclusion and recommendations presented at the end can only represent a snapshot of the current situation. Also, for an exploratory research strategy, it is often difficult to generate clear-cut results. Further research on the topic, including future market developments and applications, will be necessary for many years to come. For a true analysis and comparison of tokenized and traditional real estate investments and transactions, the market will need to mature further.

Chapter 2
Technological Background

Before diving into the topic of tokenization in real estate, the underlying technological background is presented. The chapter starts with an academic literature review of blockchain technology. Then the broad mechanics of distributed ledger technology, blockchain, smart contracts, and tokenization are summarized and explained. They are the core elements needed for the tokenization of real estate, explaining them first ensures a sound basis and understanding for the following research and work.

2.1 Literature Review: Blockchain Technology

There has been a fair amount of academic research on the topic of blockchain technology. However, as this chapter only serves as a basis for the following topic on tokenization in real estate, the review of academic papers on blockchain technology is kept brief. It serves to provide an overview of the most important topics discussed, includes well-reviewed papers in the field, and ensures the validity and integrity of this paper.

When talking about blockchain it is only logical to start with Nakamoto's 'Bitcoin: A peer-to-peer electronic cash system' (Nakamoto, 2008), the paper which introduced the concept of blockchain and Bitcoin to the world. In the paper, Nakamoto established the current inefficiencies in the financial transaction market and proposed to use blockchain and Bitcoin as an alternative solution. The main advantages lie in the disintermediation of market participants such as banks which currently serve as trusted third parties and instead allow for peer-to-peer transactions. Blockchain technology is used to ensure that there can be no double-spending: past transactions are recorded publicly, and the proof-of-work consensus mechanism verifies new transactions, making it highly impractical for an attacker to attempt to change the history of transactions in retrospect. In short, cryptographic

E. Schmid et al., *Tokenization in Real Estate*, SpringerBriefs in Finance,
https://doi.org/10.1007/978-3-031-55810-8_2

proof would substitute for trusted intermediaries and Bitcoin would serve as a new digital currency.

Following Nakamoto's introduction a new field of research was introduced; however, research was limited at first. In 2016 Yli-Huumo et al. (2016) reviewed the academic research which had been completed thus far with a focus on the technical perspective on blockchain and found 41 relevant primary papers. The authors established that most papers had focused on Bitcoin as opposed to on other potential areas of applications. Also, most research had focused on addressing current security and privacy issues of blockchain while leaving out scalability challenges. Many of the proposed solutions to security and privacy issues had, furthermore, been presented as theoretical ideas and lacked concreteness.

Zheng et al. (2017) provided a comprehensive but well-summarized overview of blockchain technology in their paper. They started by illustrating blockchain architecture in detail and describing the key characteristics associated with blockchain technology (decentralization, persistency, anonymity, and auditability). They further distinguished between public, private, and consortium blockchains and reviewed different consensus algorithms. Finally, they shed light on some of the current challenges (scalability, privacy leakage, selfish mining) and developments (blockchain testing, stopping the tendency to centralization, big data analytics, blockchain applications). Their work served as a source for explaining blockchain technology in the next chapter of this paper.

Nofer et al. (2017) also cited the work by Zheng et al. (2017) and used their illustration to explain blockchain architecture. Similarly, they provided an overview of blockchain technology. They further mentioned how smart contracts have regained popularity thanks to blockchain technology. They also pointed out alternative areas of blockchain application outside the financial industry, such as the insurance industry, notary, or music industry.

Based on the research by, amongst others, Yli-Huumo et al. (2016), Nofer et al. (2017) and Risius and Spohrer (2017) found that most academic research had focused on reviewing and improving technical details of blockchain technology such as protocols, as well as on cryptocurrencies, primarily Bitcoin. However, considering the unique characteristics of blockchain technology, especially in combination with smart contracts, they decided to thoroughly map out research that had been conducted in other areas of application. The authors created a framework to guide further advances and urged researchers to push beyond current blockchain systems and applications and include a focus on how blockchain can create true value and on its potential in a management context.

In line with preceding research, Maull et al. (2017) also identified the potential disruptiveness of this new technology, however, chose to research the overarching distributed ledger technology (DLT) out of which blockchain only represents one type. They found that the key characteristics (benefits) of DLT lie in the distributed nature of the ledger, which is based on a shared consensus between participants of the network as opposed to on trusted third parties. The immutability of the ledger coupled with transparency allows for the removal of information asymmetries. Especially in combination with smart contracts, disruptive solutions could be developed in the future. According to Maull et al. (2017), DLTs could potentially change many of the current business models in the financial industry and contribute to the concept of a sharing economy.

Zheng et al. (2018) decided to add to their previous work a year later. While the first part of the paper remained similar, the authors extended their research on the possible application areas of blockchain. They identified five main areas: finance (e.g., peer-to-peer financial market), internet of things (IoT, e.g., increase safety and privacy), public and social service (e.g., land registers), reputation system (counteract the falsification of personal reputation records, e.g., in academics), and security and privacy (e.g., improve infrastructure against attackers or protect sensitive personal data). They then continued by reviewing the same challenges and developments which had been identified previously with an addition on the topics of smart contracts and artificial intelligence (AI). Thanks to blockchain, the two concepts could be developed further and even be used in combination with each other to solve some of the technical issues of blockchain. An example is given where AI could be used to create an intelligent oracle to test whether the conditions of a smart contract have been met, omitting the need for a third-party provider. The authors concluded by stating that a further paper specifically on the topic of smart contracts would follow in the future. They followed through on that statement and the respective paper (Zheng et al., 2020) served as a valuable source for Sect. 2.4 on smart contracts.

While Zheng et al. (2017) roughly categorized blockchains into public, private, and consortium blockchains, Wüst and Gervais (2018) categorized them into permissionless and permissioned blockchains and centralized databases. Permissionless blockchains include, for example, Bitcoin and Ethereum and allow anyone to join the network as a reader (can observe and carry out transactions on the blockchain) and writer (is involved in the extension of the blockchain, meaning the consensus protocol). In a permissioned blockchain, a central entity decides on who can join the network as a reader or writer. A centralized database is what is usually in place today. The authors concluded that all three alternatives have valid applications and created a flowchart to aid in the decision-making process of which alternative is most suitable in any given case. The chart takes into account whether there is a need for data to be stored, the number of writers, the presence of a trusted third party, levels of trust in the writers, and the need for verification of new data. Generally, a blockchain only makes sense when there are multiple individuals, who do not trust each other and cannot agree on a trusted third party but want to interact with each other and together continue to adapt a shared system.

Similar to Maull et al. (2017) and Rauchs et al. (2018) decided to focus their research on the overarching topic of DLT. They started by establishing, in detail, a common basis for the definition of DLT as well as related terminology and processes as they had observed a multitude of misconceptions and discrepancies amongst academic research. They, furthermore, explained that a DLT system is made up of three independent core layers: protocol, network, and data. The protocol determines how the system operates; it is a clearly defined set of software-defined rules. The network refers to the (interconnected) actors and processes which implement said protocol. The data layer refers both to what data is stored in the DLT and how that data is and has been processed. There is a hierarchy in place for these layers in that same order, with the protocol layer being the foundational layer. A change in the protocol can, therefore, impact the network and data layer and even override decisions. Each DLT can create the three layers following its individual objectives, there is no one perfect DLT architecture and certain trade-offs will usually have to be accepted. A typical trade-off is choosing a less 'ideal' level of (de-) centralization for certain components in the different layers in exchange for performance such as increased efficiency. The authors also stated that an entirely decentralized system is almost unattainable in practice. They then analysed and compared different DLT systems based on the three layers and their individual components and processes and found that not all systems were in line with the established characteristics of DLT. Such systems were given the term potential DLT system. Finally, they concluded that the DLT ecosystem is still in its early stages and is continuing to develop.

Yaga et al. (2018) added to the literature by composing a detailed paper on the technical basis and application of blockchain written for the general public to understand. They viewed blockchain as any other new technology, however, with a lot of hype around it. Yet, the technology itself was not well understood. The paper aimed to educate and promote the application of a blockchain network in areas where it truly is beneficial. There are still issues and limitations to be addressed within blockchain technology. Consequently, it should not be considered a one-size-fits-all solution and a potential application should be well analysed first.

Zheng et al. (2018) are cited by Monrat et al. (2019) in their paper on blockchain technology. Monrat et al. again provided a full-scale overview of blockchain technology including blockchain architecture and characteristics, the transaction process, consensus mechanisms, and potential application areas. The authors put a large focus on issues that should still be developed further: performance and scalability, privacy, interoperability, energy consumption, fairness and security, and current regulation problems. Their overall research coincided with the research of academics before them and so did their conclusions. Monrat et al. saw high potential in blockchain technology and believed the potential application areas are vast. They, however, agreed with Yaga et al. that it should only be implemented in a way where it truly adds value. As already mentioned by Zheng et al., they also suggested blockchain testing before implementing a new blockchain solution. Finally, they identified many possibilities and opportunities in the use of smart contracts in combination with blockchain. However, keeping in mind that even a small bug within the code can have disastrous results and should therefore be incorporated with caution.

As more researchers identified the possibilities that lie within the blockchain technology, more research on specific applications followed. This includes the research by Shahnaz et al. (2019) on the use of electronic health records, Chang and Chen (2020) on supply chain management, and Upadhyay et al. (2021) on the potential impact on a circular economy.

Further academic research on blockchain technology, its potential and applications as well as challenges is expected to be carried out in the future. As stated at the beginning of the chapter, the above literature review only presents a selection of current research as blockchain technology is only one piece of this paper.

2.2 Distributed Ledger Technology

The term distributed ledger technology or DLT is often used synonymously with blockchain and sometimes even with Bitcoin. It is therefore important to define that blockchain is a type of distributed ledger technology. A multitude of different definitions for DLT have been made in academics, some more broad, some more technical, and others which have been considered too simplistic. Rauchs et al. (2018, pp. 20–24) reviewed the concept of DLT in detail and came up with the following definition: 'A DLT system is a system of electronic records that enables a network of independent participants to establish a consensus around the authoritative ordering of cryptographically-validated ("signed") transactions. These records are made persistent by replicating the data across multiple nodes, tamper evident by linking them by cryptographic hashes. The shared result of the reconciliation/consensus process—the "ledger"—serves as the authoritative version for these records'. The definition aimed to include the key characteristics of DLT while not excluding any of its potential future applications. It is, however, a very condensed definition. Hence, the underlying concept of DLT is explained again, in simpler words, below.

At its core, DLT is a shared record of data and is typically publicly accessible. The data is synchronized across the network and new data is added to the ledger in chronological order, however, only once it has been verified by the system. This concept allows for a decentralized system that does not rely upon an intermediary party or require trust between participants as consensus on the data in the ledger must be reached among participants. The concept is based on the assumption that there are potentially untrustworthy members in the network, however, thanks to the consensus protocol that doesn't matter, you only need to trust the consensus algorithm in place. DLT can, as a result, remove information asymmetry as one agreed-upon truth is transparently shared among all members of the network, often visible to the public. This alternative solution to storing data could remove costs and increase efficiency; however, it could also undermine business models which draw value from information asymmetries. Meanwhile, the participants themselves stay anonymous within the network, and even when adding data to the ledger only the activity itself is visible. Furthermore, the ledger is immutable and highly resistant to manipulation, enabling high data security. The unique combination of these characteristics should allow for a variety of use cases (Maull et al., 2017).

Overall, the DLT ecosystem is still in its early stages and is generally viewed as relatively immature. New systems are constantly being added resulting in an ever-evolving ecosystem (Rauchs et al., 2018, p. 92). DLT also faces a series of challenges. Here, the continuous development is aiding in implementing improvements and new application possibilities (Natarajan et al., 2017, p. 1). Academics have also mentioned the need for analysing and discussing other DLT concepts apart from blockchain. So far, however, within the real estate industry, blockchain is by far the most adopted DLT solution (Liu et al., 2020, pp. 10, 19). It will, therefore, continue to be the focus of this chapter on the technological background.

2.3 Blockchain Technology

Following the review of academic research in the field of blockchain and the general introduction of DLT, this chapter will focus specifically on blockchain technology, its underlying concept, technical aspects, potential, and challenges.

2.3.1 *Definition*

Yaga et al. (2018, p. 1) have written a detailed report on the technical basis and applications of blockchain, as has been stated in the literature review. They offer the following definition for blockchain: 'Blockchains are distributed digital ledgers of cryptographically signed transactions that are grouped into blocks. Each block is cryptographically linked to the previous one (making it tamper evident) after validation and undergoing a consensus decision. As new blocks are added, older blocks become more difficult to modify (creating tamper resistance). New blocks are replicated across copies of the ledger within the network, and any conflicts are resolved automatically using established rules'.

Following the evolution of blockchain after its introduction in 2008, Swan (2015) further classified blockchain into Blockchain 1.0, 2.0, and 3.0. Blockchain 1.0 refers to digital currencies and payments such as Bitcoin. It is the decentralization of money, enabling transparent peer-to-peer transactions. Bitcoin 2.0 refers to transactions of assets outside of cryptocurrencies (e.g., stocks, patents) and migrating data to a blockchain (e.g., passports, vehicle registrations), it is the decentralization of markets. It includes protocols, smart contracts, smart properties, decentralized applications (dApps), decentralized autonomous organizations (DAO), and decentralized autonomous corporations (DAC). Finally, Blockchain 3.0 refers to the application of blockchain outside of the financial market in the areas of, for example, health care, science, and government. It is the universal use of blockchain, fully taking advantage of the technology and all its benefits.

2.3.2 *Underlying Concept*

Currency transactions between two parties are usually carried out and controlled by a trusted third party. This creates a dependency on third-party organizations for the financial network to function smoothly. These middlemen often charge a fee for their services and the transaction is centralized around them as they oversee and control all the information involved. The idea behind blockchain is to offer an alternative to this system (Nakamoto, 2008, p. 1). To create a decentralized environment where peer-to-peer transactions are possible, data is not shared with an additional intermediary. Instead, a public ledger records all transactions and is then shared and accessible to all participants in the network, increasing transparency. Once a set of data has been added to the public ledger and verified by all participants, it cannot be modified or deleted, resulting in a high level of data integrity. At the same time, participants remain anonymous (Yli-Huumo et al., 2016, pp. 1–2).

The concept of blockchain has been described many times. The outlines composed by Zheng et al. (2018, p. 357) and Lai et al. (2020, p. 6) in particular, complement each other well and are thus both presented. Zheng et al. established four key characteristics to define blockchain, as was found during the literature review: decentralization, persistency, anonymity, and auditability. The decentralization is achieved through the facilitation of peer-to-peer transactions. Persistency refers to the correctness of the ledger as each entry has to be verified by the network. Also, members of the network can remain anonymous throughout their activities and there is no centralized entity that keeps data on each member. Finally, auditability is given as each transaction is recorded with a timestamp, members can go back and check any previous transaction. Privacy and anonymity seem to contradict the aspect of transparency at first. A completely private ledger would provide no transparency and vice versa. However, as has been explained, a blockchain can still maintain the privacy of each member's identity while offering information on the activities carried out, and on the data stored on the blockchain. Still, this does tear at the efficiency of the blockchain (Wüst & Gervais, 2018, p. 46).

Later, Lai et al. (2020, p. 6) outline the concept of blockchain with three main characteristics. Firstly, a blockchain's ledger is distributed, meaning it is stored and accessible throughout the entire network. Secondly, it operates on a decentralized basis and is not controlled by a single entity, so the system does not require or rely on trust between participants. Thirdly, the blockchain is immutable. Once data has been added and verified it is almost impossible to change. As a result, a census between all participants is created on what is true.

In other words, blockchain is an alternative solution to storing data. In a technical sense, it is typically described as a chain consisting of multiple blocks in chronological order. The chain is continuous and ever extendable with new blocks. Each block contains data to be stored such as past transactions. Together, the blockchain can present a complete ledger of all past transactions made between participants in the network. It is, therefore, considered a DLT solution. Apart from increasing transparency and ensuring the integrity and security of data, blockchain has the potential to both save costs and increase efficiency (Zheng et al., 2017, p. 557). Furthermore, the network as a whole still works even if a node (participant) breaks down, meaning that it is not necessary to trust the other participants but only the entirety of the network (Nofer et al., 2017, p. 184).

Applications of blockchain have been primarily focused on the finance industry, this is due to the technology having been introduced simultaneously with Bitcoin. However, the technology has the potential to be effectively applied in areas outside of cryptocurrency and the financial industry as well. This potential has been identified by many and the application of blockchain has been suggested for the healthcare industry, energy industry, manufacturing, government, and distribution. Crowdfunding, identity management, electronic voting, and the management of public records have also been mentioned to potentially benefit from the use of blockchain (Monrat et al., 2019, p. 117134). These alternative areas of application mostly benefit from one key advantage of blockchain, its security characteristics: asymmetric cryptography and consensus algorithms are incorporated into the blockchain to ensure the security and accuracy of data (Zheng et al., 2017, p. 557).

2.3.3 Blockchain Architecture

Before illustrating the architecture of a blockchain, a further distinction is made. A blockchain can be roughly categorized as either a public, private, or consortium blockchain. Their differences are presented in Fig. 2.1. A public blockchain is accessible by anyone interested, and added data is verified by all participants, it is permissionless. Due to the many participants, it is hard to tamper with, however, this also decreases efficiency. A private blockchain, on the other hand, is controlled by one entity that decides on the consensus algorithm, decides who gets to access the data on the blockchain and who can participate, it is permissioned. These limitations increase the efficiency of the blockchain, however, also make it easier to be tampered with. The centralized characteristic is also not in line with the initial concept of blockchain. The consortium blockchain forms a middle ground. A selected set of nodes are responsible to reach consensus. The blockchain can, therefore, be considered partly centralized and is also still considered permissioned. The limitation, however, again increases efficiency while decreasing security (Zheng et al., 2017, p. 559). An alternative categorization of blockchain is to simply distinguish between permissionless blockchains and permissioned blockchains (Wüst & Gervais, 2018).

Having defined the different types of blockchains, the make-up of a single block is illustrated next. Each block is made up of a block header and a block body. In addition to the data, which is stored in the body, each block contains seven elements in the block header (Zheng et al., 2018, p. 356). The structure of a block header can be seen in Fig. 2.2.

Each block includes the block version, that indicates which validation rules are to follow. It also includes a hash, a unique value which identifies each block and

Property	Public blockchain	Consortium blockchain	Private blockchain
Consensus determination	All miners	Selected set of nodes	One organization
Read permission	Public	Could be public or restricted	Could be public or restricted
Immutability	Nearly impossible to tamper	Could be tampered	Could be tampered
Efficiency	Low	High	High
Centralized	No	Partial	Yes
Consensus process	Permissionless	Permissioned	Permissioned

Fig. 2.1 *Public, Consortium, and Private Blockchains. Note.* From Zheng et al. (2017), p. 559. doi: 10.1109/BigDataCongress.2017.85

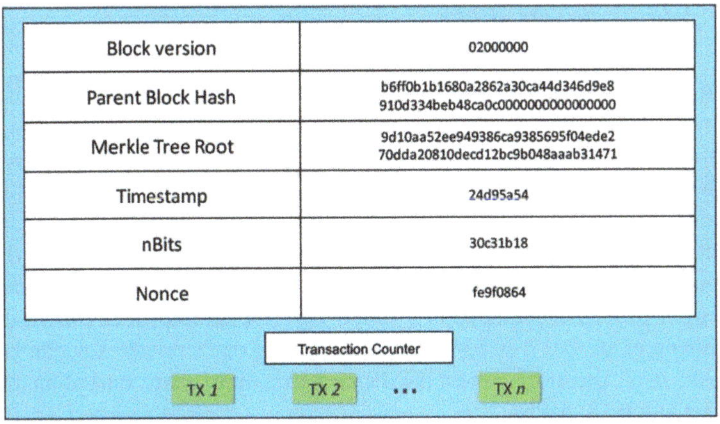

Fig. 2.2 *Structure Block Header. Note.* From Zheng et al. (2018), p. 356. doi: 10.1504/IJWGS.2018.095647

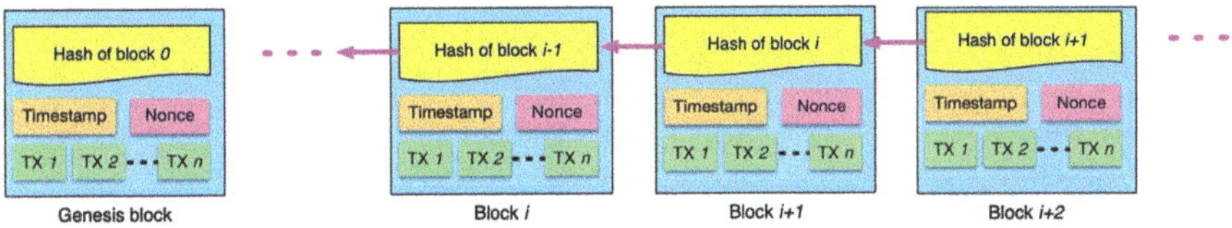

Fig. 2.3 *Structure Blockchain. Note.* From Zheng et al. (2018), p. 355. doi: 10.1504/IJWGS.2018.095647

its (transaction) data. The hash is also known as the Merkle tree root hash as it includes and identifies all data in the block. Or in other words, each individual transaction in the block has its own hash, and the Merkle tree root hash summarizes and includes them all. The block header also repeats the hash of its parent block, or the block, which was added immediately before it in the blockchain. Hence, each block references to its preceding block. The very first block, also known as the genesis block, does not include this element. If the information in the block is changed, the Merkle tree root hash changes as well. The next block now references to a hash that does not exist anymore. It and all the following blocks are rendered mute. The timestamp on the block allows one to pinpoint the exact time at which the transaction took place. nBits refers to the current hashing target and is shown in a compact format. The nonce (number only used once) is used to compute the hash value of the block during the verification process (Zheng et al., 2018, p. 355). The block body includes a transaction count that shows the number of transactions stored within the block as well as the transactions themselves. The number of transactions that can be stored in one block depends on the size of the block as well as on the size of the transactions. Together, the various verified blocks build a blockchain. A visualization of a blockchain can be seen in Fig. 2.3 (Zheng et al., 2018, p. 355).

2.3.4 Adding a New Block

Before a new block can be added a transaction needs to take place. To ensure a secure transaction for both parties, a digital signature is used. A digital signature requires asymmetric cryptography. Each node has two keys, a public and a private one. When digitally signing a transaction, node A encrypts the transaction hash value using their private key. The transaction data and the encrypted hash value are then sent to node B. This is known as the signing phase. Node B also derives the hash value from the transaction and checks it against the one they have been sent, decrypting it first by using node A's public key. This is known as the verification phase (Zheng et al., 2017, p. 558). Securely storing one's private key can be a difficult task, it is, therefore, often outsourced to a third-party custodian provider (Rauchs et al., 2018, p. 28).

When a transaction has successfully taken place, another set of steps follows to add the transaction to the blockchain. When first introducing blockchain technology, Nakamoto (2008, p. 3) established six steps to do so when using the proof-of-work (PoW) consensus mechanism. The six steps are:

1. 'New transactions are broadcast to all nodes.
2. Each node collects new transactions into a block.
3. Each node works on finding a difficult proof-of-work for its block.
4. When a node finds a proof-of-work, it broadcasts the block to all nodes.
5. Nodes accept the block only if all transactions in it are valid and not already spent.
6. Nodes express their acceptance of the block by working on creating the next block in the chain, using the hash of the accepted block as the previous hash'.

Rauchs et al. (2018, pp. 26, 63) also analysed how a new transaction is processed within the network. Their explanation of how new transaction data is treated and stored following broadcasting complements Nakamoto's steps well. The process as established by Rauchs et al. can be seen in Fig. 2.4. First, validating nodes store transactions that are yet to be confirmed in their logs, at this point the logs of various

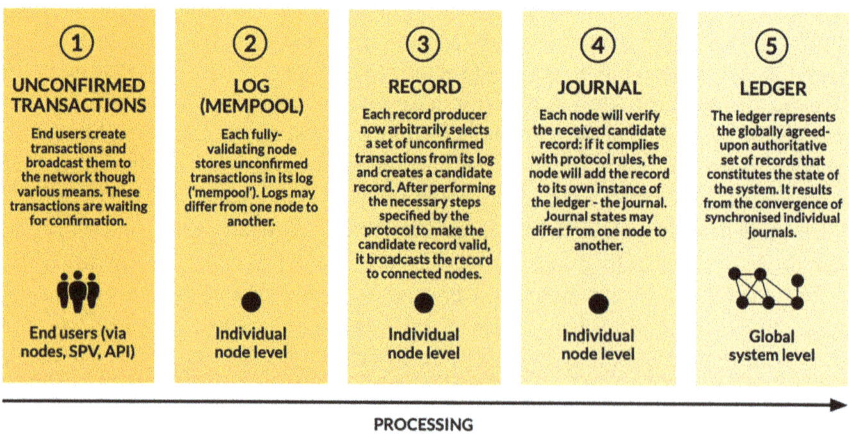

Fig. 2.4 *Blockchain Transaction Process. Note.* From Rauchs et al. (2018), *Cambridge Centre for Alternative Finance Reports*, p. 26 (https://ssrn.com/abstract=3230013)

nodes can look different. The nodes then select transactions in their logs and perform the computational steps to validate them. If successful, the new valid record is broadcasted to other nodes. These nodes again check the validity of the new record and if they comply with protocol store them in their journals. Again, the journal of one node can momentarily differ from the journal of another. Finally, the ledger shows the globally agreed-upon set of validated and verified records and is a result of nodes synchronizing their personal journals. These steps are a crucial part of blockchain and other DLT systems as it allows for the participants of a network to individually audit new data.

The computational work necessary to validate a new block makes use of the different elements of the block header, as described above. With Bitcoin's PoW consensus strategy the nodes in the network are computing the changing hash value in the block header by using and adjusting the nonce. The target value must be equal to or smaller than the defined threshold nBits. Once a node is successful, the network confirms the correctness of the value, and the respective transactions can be added as a new block. Computing hash values to add new blocks is known as mining. The nodes doing the computations are called miners (Yaga et al., 2018, p. 19). As the computation needed for authentication is a time-consuming process, the strategy includes an incentive mechanism where the successful node is given Bitcoin as a reward. In a scenario where more than one node finds a suitable nonce at the same time, the network might be conflicted about which block to verify and add. As a result, branches, also known as forks, can be created. Generally, the longer branch is considered the authentic one and is continued (Zheng et al., 2018, p. 359).

PoW has a series of drawbacks. It limits the addition of new blocks as the miners need to be given time to do the computations (in the case of Bitcoin one block can be added every 10 min, limiting the number of transactions to around 6–10 per second). Also, many nodes in the network are working on the same computation, so a large amount of energy is needed for each block. Other mechanisms have therefore been developed such as proof-of-stake (PoS). Here, one node is chosen to carry out the computation. However, nodes which own more of the respective cryptocurrencies are more likely to be chosen, as it is believed that they are less likely to harm the blockchain considering their large stake. This concept has not always been considered fair and alternative methods to choosing the node have been suggested. In PoS, carrying out the computation is known as forging, the chosen node is called the validator. Other distributed consensus algorithms include Practical Byzantine Fault Tolerance (PBFT), delegated proof-of-stake (DPoS), Ripple, and Tendermint. All carry their advantages and disadvantages (Zheng et al., 2017, pp. 559–561).

2.3.5 Challenges

With any innovation, there are challenges to overcome. The literature review on blockchain technology has shown that experts largely agree on the biggest issues which are yet to be solved. They are listed and explained in this section of the paper.

Scalability: Blockchains often deal with scalability or congestion issues. Naturally, this is of concern for entities wishing to implement a blockchain solution. Developers often have to choose between the performance and size of the network. A public network such as Bitcoin can include a considerable number of participants and is, therefore, well scalable. However, it also has a vast number of messages and exchanges happening between its nodes, impacting the throughput and latency of the network negatively: Bitcoin's PoW consensus mechanism can only add a new block every 10 min, limiting the number of transactions to around 6–10 transaction per second, a lot less than other technologies in use today. While these limitations were designed to increase security, they also hinder the wide usage of the technology. Participants, furthermore, often prefer larger transactions as they are rewarded with a higher fee, causing delays for many smaller transactions (Monrat et al., 2019, p. 117145). A consortium or private blockchain can often process new data better and add blocks more efficiently as there are fewer nodes in the network but is instead limited in its overall size and might lose part of its decentralization characteristic. As a result of scalability issues, the DCS (decentralization, consistency, scalability) triangle has been created. It states that blockchain can always only meet two of the three requirements (Monrat et al., 2019, p. 117145). There have been specific research addressing the issue and suggesting a range of possible solutions, for example, by Zhou et al. (2020).

Security: The concept of blockchain is based on malicious nodes being part of the network but not impacting the integrity of the ledger as they are outnumbered, and new data is only added to a ledger if verified by a majority. It is, therefore, generally agreed upon that a malicious node or a group of malicious nodes would need to gain control over 51% of the network's hash rate/computing power to issue an attack. This is often an unlikely scenario, especially in public networks with a vast number of members. However, selfish mining can cause security issues even when less than 51% of the network decides to collude. Should selfish miners be successful in hiding their newly mined blocks and their branch would upon the reveal be the longer branch, the work of honest miners would be wasted, and potentially wrongful data would be added as the network would accept the longer branch as the right one. Also, the selfish miners would generate more revenue as they are mining without competition, attracting rational miners to join them. Overall, however, most big blockchains have proven to be resilient against attacks (Zheng et al., 2018, pp. 368–369; Monrat et al., 2019, p. 117147).

Privacy: A blockchain is generally considered secure, allowing members to remain anonymous by using a generated address as opposed to personal details when participating in the network. However, there have been reported cases of private data leakage, for instance, when pseudonyms could be linked to IP addresses. Also, while the true identity of participants should remain unknown, the transactions they carry out can be seen by everyone in the network. Should a node repeatedly transact with a particular second node in the network, identifiable by the generated address, a relationship could become apparent. Proposed solutions to the issue include carrying out transactions via a third node to hide the relationship (Zheng et al., 2018, pp. 367–368; Monrat et al., 2019, p. 117146).

Energy Consumption: The PoW algorithm used for Bitcoin requires an extensive amount of electrical energy as many nodes are looking for the right nonce simultaneously. However, only one solution is needed in the end. Also, Bitcoin is contributing highly to global carbon emissions as power plants in China supplying the electricity needed to mine new Bitcoin blocks are fuelled with coal (Monrat et al., 2019, p. 117147).

Consensus algorithms: It has been established that the PoW consensus algorithm carries considerable challenges such as high energy consumption or selfish mining. As has been mentioned earlier, alternatives have been developed and proposed as a result. One of the most known is the PoS mechanism, to which the Ethereum network is currently switching, a move that has been years in the making (Castor, 2022). PoS is considered a lot more energy efficient (Zheng et al., 2018, p. 360). However, PoS can come with its own concerns. One of them is that the nodes chosen to validate a new block are chosen based on their stake in the network, making the rich richer. This can also lead to increased centralization (Monrat et al., 2019, pp. 117139, 117141). Generally, all consensus mechanisms come with their advantages and disadvantages. Innovations within the field of consensus algorithms are, therefore, frequent and usually aimed at increasing transaction speed, security, and/or becoming more energy efficient.

Interoperability: Implementing blockchain solutions is becoming increasingly more popular across a variety of fields, as has been illustrated so far. Ideally, these blockchains should be able to collaborate and interact with each other. However, there is a lack of standard protocol enabling interoperability. While it allows developers freedom in the programming of different blockchains and platforms, it hinders the development of a larger connected blockchain ecosystem (Monrat et al., 2019, p. 117146). Creating an interoperable ecosystem is important in the context of tokenization in real estate as well, as is discussed at the end of Sect. 3.4.

Uncertainty around regulations: Another hindrance in the further development of the blockchain ecosystem and the implementation of blockchain solutions are uncertainties around regulations. Using blockchain solutions can, consequently, come with additional risks and is even banned in some jurisdictions (Monrat et al., 2019, p. 117147). When discussing the implementation of blockchain and tokens in the real estate industry later in the paper, it will become apparent that regulatory challenges are among the main issues within the field (see Sects. 3.4 and 3.5).

Risks for investors: There are also risks for investors to consider. So far, digital assets such as cryptocurrencies have shown high volatility due to uncertainties or media hypes, for example (Lapin, 2021). Furthermore, there have been a series of scams. According to Chainalysis' (2022) *Crypto Crime Report* (2022), $7.8 billion worth of cryptocurrency was taken from investors in 2021. Investments should, therefore, be done with caution.

Generally, all the presented issues have been addressed by experts on the topic, and various solutions have been proposed, tried out, and/or implemented. Changes and further developments in the technological details of blockchain are happening continuously. The above explanations of the challenges in this section focused on explaining the underlying issues as opposed to analysing potential solutions as such an analysis would require a lot more in-depth research and go beyond the scope of this paper.

2.4 Smart Contracts

The literature review showed that smart contracts are regularly discussed in the context of blockchain and many researchers see great potential in their application (Monrat et al., 2019; Nofer et al., 2017; Risius & Spohrer, 2017). The reason for this is that the creation of blockchain technology offered a simplified basis for the application of smart contracts (Nofer et al., 2017, p. 185). Smart contracts were first introduced by Szabo in 1997 in his article *Formalizing and Securing Relationships on Public Networks*. He presented how smart contracts can be implemented digitally to increase efficiency and security while decreasing costs compared to traditional, paper-based contracts. More specifically, Szabo (1997, p. 3) stated that 'Smart contracts utilize protocols and user interfaces to facilitate all steps of the contracting process. This gives us new ways to formalize and secure digital relationships which are far more functional than their inanimate paper-based ancestors. [...] The basic idea behind smart contracts is that many kinds of contractual clauses can be embedded in the hardware and software we deal with, in such a way as to make a breach of contract expensive for the breacher'. In other words, smart contracts are programmes that automatically execute the contract clauses when pre-defined conditions are met.

In a technical sense, smart contracts are implemented on top of the blockchain as the contract clauses are translated into executable computer programmes, guaranteeing the enforcement of the contract in a predictable manner. The lifecycle of smart contracts can be divided into four phases. In the creation phase, the involved parties negotiate the terms of the contract. These terms are then converted into computer software. The deployment of the smart contracts on top of the blockchain then follows. Here it is important to mention that a smart contract cannot be changed once it is on the blockchain, a new contract would have to be created instead. Also, anyone within the network can view the smart contracts once incorporated into the blockchain. The execution of the smart contracts then follows, assuming that the pre-defined conditions have been met. When the execution of a smart contract has been triggered, the following activity is validated by the network and recorded in the ledger as would be the case with any other transaction on a blockchain as well. Finally, the completion of smart contracts encompasses the update of the ledger and each node's journal to include recent activities (Zheng et al., 2020, pp. 3–4).

The main advantages of smart contracts lie in the reduction of risks, as the immutability of blockchain protects smart contracts from being altered following the deployment phase. Also, as all activities are recorded on the blockchain and duplicated throughout the whole network the system is considered traceable and auditable. Smart contracts can also enable cutting down administration and service costs, as they are triggered automatically and can be applied in a decentralized system.

This allows bypassing intermediaries such as lawyers or bankers to securely handle and carry out transactions between two parties. The resulting improved peer-to-peer affairs can greatly increase the efficiency of business processes. There is a range of fields that could potentially benefit from the implementation of smart contracts: IoT (e.g., to set up a DAC), distributed system security (to help set in place security measures in computer networks, e.g., filter traffic from malicious users), finance (to reduce administrative efforts and costs while increasing efficiency, e.g., in the mortgage loan industry), data provenance (to ensure data quality in, e.g., public health by storing meta-data on the origin, derivation and transformation of that data), sharing economy (e.g., decentralize sharing economy platforms), and the public sector (e.g., to help build e-voting systems) (Zheng et al., 2020, pp. 12–16).

As with blockchain technology, smart contracts also face challenges. These challenges include the readability of the smart contract code. While the code is accessible to all nodes it is written in programming language making it difficult to understand and audit. Also, as the code of a smart contract can't be adjusted once deployed it is important to thoroughly check it for bugs. However, this can be difficult due to the complexity of smart contracts, and a variety of methods have been developed and suggested to simplify the process. These methods should also take into consideration how the smart contract might behave in connection with other smart contracts as well as the reliability of the execution environment (Zheng et al., 2020, pp. 4–6). Bugs have caused disastrous results in the past, so final implementation should not be done lightly (Monrat et al., 2019, p. 117148). Further considerations should include the trustworthiness of oracles. Oracles signify agents/entities which find and verify data outside of the blockchain and forward them to the smart contract, as the blockchain itself is an isolated network and cannot pull in data from an external system. However, smart contracts cannot check for the source or quality of the information they are provided. The issue of 'garbage in, garbage out' persists (Liu et al., 2020, p. 18). Execution efficiency has also been said to be challenging. Smart contracts are executed by the network one after the other, however, as execution can take time delays can be the result, limiting the performance of the network. Privacy concerns as described in Sect. 2.3, furthermore, remain for transactions triggered by smart contracts and should be addressed as well (Zheng et al., 2020, pp. 8–9). Finally, regulatory issues can arise with the implementation of smart contracts, especially across borders. In the case of a breach, legal consequences might not be clearly defined. Also, the acceptance/legality of digital signatures has not yet been established in many jurisdictions (Liu et al., 2020, p. 18).

2.5 Tokenization

Following the introduction on the topics of DLT, blockchain, and smart contracts, the concept of tokenization will be briefly presented in this subchapter. When referring to tokenization in real estate, a primary application of blockchain and often also

<table>
<tr><td rowspan="3">Purpose Parameters</td><td>Class</td><td colspan="3">Coin / Cryptocurrency</td><td colspan="2">Utility Token</td><td colspan="3">Tokenised Security</td></tr>
<tr><td>Function</td><td colspan="3">Asset-Based Token</td><td colspan="2">Usage Token</td><td colspan="3">Work Token</td></tr>
<tr><td>Role</td><td>Right</td><td colspan="2">Value Exchange</td><td>Toll</td><td>Reward</td><td colspan="2">Currency</td><td>Earnings</td></tr>
<tr><td rowspan="3">Governance Parameters</td><td>Representation</td><td colspan="3">Digital</td><td colspan="2">Physical</td><td colspan="3">Legal</td></tr>
<tr><td>Supply</td><td colspan="2">Schedule-based</td><td colspan="2">Pre-mined, scheduled distribution</td><td colspan="2">Pre-mined, one-off distribution</td><td colspan="2">Discretionary</td></tr>
<tr><td>Incentive System</td><td colspan="2">Enter Platform</td><td colspan="2">Use Platform</td><td colspan="2">Stay Long-Term</td><td colspan="2">Leave Platform</td></tr>
<tr><td rowspan="5">Functional Parameters</td><td>Spendability</td><td colspan="4">Spendable</td><td colspan="4">Non-Spendable</td></tr>
<tr><td>Tradability</td><td colspan="4">Tradable</td><td colspan="4">Non-Tradable</td></tr>
<tr><td>Burnability</td><td colspan="4">Burnable</td><td colspan="4">Non-Burnable</td></tr>
<tr><td>Expirability</td><td colspan="4">Expirable</td><td colspan="4">Non-Expirable</td></tr>
<tr><td>Fungibility</td><td colspan="4">Fungible</td><td colspan="4">Non-Fungible</td></tr>
<tr><td rowspan="2">Technical Parameters</td><td>Layer</td><td colspan="3">Blockchain (Native)</td><td colspan="2">Protocol (Non-Native)</td><td colspan="3">Application (dApp)</td></tr>
<tr><td>Chain</td><td colspan="2">New Chain new Code</td><td colspan="2">New Chain, forked Code</td><td colspan="2">Forked Chain, forked Code</td><td colspan="2">Issued on top of a protocol</td></tr>
</table>

Fig. 2.5 *Overview Token Classification. Note.* From Oliveira et al. (2018), *39th International Conference on Information Systems*, San Francisco, USA, p. 9 (https://www.researchgate.net/publication/328162731)

smart contracts is largely implied. Having covered these topics, the concept of tokenization is briefly outlined. A detailed explanation of tokenization in real estate is then presented in Chap. 3.

The concept and process of tokenization can be described as the conversion of a tangible or intangible asset into a token. In simple terms, a digital token is a piece of software with a unique reference either to the ownership of an asset or to specific rights attached. It enables the digital ownership, transfer, and storage of an asset. Tokenization does not necessarily have to run on a DLT or blockchain but doing so allows participants to take advantage of the safety and transparency characteristics of blockchain technology (Stefanoski et al., 2020, p. 12). Having said that, it is apparent that a token can fulfil a range of different purposes as its ability to represent something digitally can be useful in many cases. Consequently, it is not surprising that a token can also have a range of different characteristics.

Figure 2.5 by Oliveira et al. (2018, p. 9) shows a very detailed overview of said possibilities.

A tokenized real estate asset can *generally* be characterized as:

- *Purpose parameters*: An asset-based security token potentially generating earnings.
- *Governance parameters*: Representation of a physical asset in the form of a token to incentivize the investment in said real estate asset, in this case, to enter the platform.

- *Functional parameters*: Real estate tokens are usually non-spendable, tradable, non-burnable, non-expirable, and fungible. However, there could be deviations to these classifications, for example, when not the asset itself is tokenized but an intermediate form of ownership is in place and investors buy tokenized bonds instead which come with a maturity date.
- *Technical parameters*: Depend on the chosen set-up of the blockchain.

Further definitions of tokenization in real estate specifically as well as of the different types of tokens relevant for this paper are presented in Sect. 3.2.

Chapter 3
Tokenization in Real Estate

In the following chapter, the main topic of the paper, tokenization in real estate, is discussed. Similar to Chaps. 2 and 3 will first present a review of the academic literature which has been published on the topic so far. Then, the different types of tokens are defined, and potential applications are presented. This is followed by examining current challenges as well as the legal basis in Switzerland. Finally, the newest developments are reviewed, including an international outlook.

3.1 Literature Review: Tokenization in Real Estate

Tokenization in real estate is still a fairly new topic for academics to focus on. As a result, the available literature on the topic is limited. Still, the most important pieces of work published so far will be reviewed in this chapter.

Veuger (2017) took the concept of disruption (as defined by Steven Sinofsky with the four phases: disruption, evolution, convergence, and re-imagination) and applied it to blockchain technology and the real estate industry. Just like Amazon, Zalando, and Uber managed to disrupt their industries with new business concepts based on digital technology, the author believed that blockchain could be the underlying technology for companies to disrupt the real estate industry. Veuger saw the added value of using blockchain in better and more efficient real estate transaction processes, increased data transparency, and the potential for new developments in the mortgage market. However, at this point, there were still many uncertainties around the future application of blockchain and its success. For it to be a real game-changer, the author concluded that trust in the blockchain technology by market participants must first be given.

Two years later, Sull and Baum (2019) analysed and explained, in detail, what an entirely digitalized real estate transaction could look like. They concluded that the digitalization of the land register is the single most important step before digital

E. Schmid et al., *Tokenization in Real Estate*, SpringerBriefs in Finance,
https://doi.org/10.1007/978-3-031-55810-8_3

transactions can be brought to the masses. This, however, requires huge efforts and costs from authorities and landowners, and they raised the question of which party will be the pushing force behind completing this endeavour. Overall, they were convinced that the development of the technology will outpace the implementation by the market.

Meanwhile, the paper by the MIT Digital Currency Initiative (Smith et al., 2019) focused on the potential benefits of applying tokenization in commercial real estate assets. They concluded that significant value can be derived by not only applying blockchain and tokenization in real estate investment and trading but also by applying them to the underlying asset. Meaning, digitalizing the real estate asset and its property data. This could greatly improve transparency around, for example, the property's value drivers. Along with the potential benefits the authors also mentioned the potential negative impacts some market participants could experience as a result of changing business processes. Brokers, law firms, debt servicers, or large institutional investors, for example, might need to adjust their services.

The second article by Baum (2020) mentioned the MIT report when defining the concept of tokenization in real estate and when reviewing the potential benefits and challenges of tokenization in real estate. Baum, furthermore, offered a great, in-depth overview and analysis of tokenization in real estate in the global market. They also reviewed the work and recommendations of a range of other experts and, as a result, offered insightful conclusions. Most importantly, they argued that the current focus should lie on familiarizing the market with blockchain and tokenization. To do so, they recommended using intermediate structures which are then fractionalized and tokenized as opposed to focusing on fractionalizing single real estate assets. The author specifically saw the most potential in using funds, as the legal basis for their use already exists in many countries.

Berentsen and Markheim (2020) came to similar conclusions in their paper. They described the same potential benefits of tokenization; increased liquidity through the possibility of trading 24/7 without intermediaries, flexibility through the use of smart contracts which theoretically allow for the inclusion of any code or rule, transparency as the blockchain is accessible by anyone in the network, and finally security thanks to the immutability of the data on a blockchain. Tokens can, furthermore, offer an alternative to traditional ways of raising capital at significantly less cost. They compared the implementation to the internet. The internet almost reduced the cost of communication (through, e.g., e-mail or WhatsApp) to zero. Cryptocurrencies and tokens could do the same with the cost of transferring value. However, the regulatory uncertainties are largely hindering market participants from taking advantage of these benefits in practice.

In line with Konashevych (2020) also identified the need for digitalizing land registries as one of the biggest hurdles to overcome. They argued that real estate owners should have the right to choose how to manage their property ownership and rights. This would establish a basis for free competition and allow for the creation of better land registry services in a decentralized manner. Owners could create a token that represents their property rights, a title token, and choose on which blockchain they would like to store it. Apart from being slow and bureaucratic,

Konashevych saw further difficulties in a centralized land register controlled by the government, it allows for the abuse of power and corruption. Instead, he proposed that the government should be in charge of facilitating a cross-blockchain infrastructure to incorporate the blockchains of the various providers, including setting security standards through the incorporation of the so-called smart laws.

Liu et al. (2020) published a detailed review of the potential of distributed ledger technology (DLT) in the field of real estate as part of RICS Research. They established that DLT has the potential to disrupt the industry; however, there are still technical and legal challenges to overcome. Furthermore, based on their survey, there is still a lot of uncertainty and misunderstanding in the market. They came to the conclusion that the different stakeholders and participants in the market will need to work together, ideally with guidance from the government, to successfully apply the new solutions in a wide manner. Use cases so far are not able to harvest many of the potential benefits and are basically another form of crowdfunding for real estate investments. Still, the potential of DLT should not be disregarded. Market participants who are worried about their future role in the value chain are recommended to focus on consultancy-based roles. Finally, they mentioned the need to analyse further DLT solutions apart from blockchain.

A couple of articles have focused on the topic of commercial real estate (CRE). Oppendaker and Wouda (Wouda & Opdenakker, 2019), for example, focused on CRE transactions, which they deemed are often time-consuming and inefficient, mostly due to inadequate market transparency. They conducted expert interviews to find out which elements in the transaction process were causing the issues and then created a blockchain application to overcome these difficulties. The application changes how physical and contractual data is structured and stored while simultaneously verifying said data. This increases the data quality and, as a result, increases transparency and trust during a transaction process. They further suggested that the digitalized record of data could function as the foundation of tokenization in real estate. Nijland and Veuger (2019) added to this topic, describing real estate assets as heterogeneous and immobile, causing more expensive and complex transactions. They also found the due diligence phase to be most suited for the application of blockchain. A more secure data sharing could be achieved with blockchain and third parties potentially bypassed. However, they assessed the technology to still be in the development phase and, therefore, not yet ready for broad application in the industry. Pankratov et al. (2020) also reviewed the application of blockchain to the real estate transaction process and found that they could be carried out safer, faster, and cheaper with blockchain. This is due to the increased transparency when storing property data on a blockchain and the consensus mechanism, which makes it difficult to tamper with data. They, furthermore, estimated a broad application of blockchain technology in the market within the next 6–7 years.

Finally, there are of course further articles that have been written on the topic. Hoxha and Sadiku (2019) asked around 1000 professionals in Kosovo about their views on the implementation of blockchain technology in real estate and its potential benefits for real estate transactions. Most respondents reported a positive view towards blockchain and stated transparency, cost reduction, and security as the main benefits, in that order. Meanwhile, Jyotsna and Gampala (2020) and Shabbir (2021) largely agreed with the above-mentioned experts on the drawbacks of traditional real estate investment and transactions (such as illiquidity and high costs) as well as on the potential benefits that tokenization holds (increased speed and transparency). Shabbir further mentioned similar challenges which still need to be overcome to implement tokenization on a large scale, especially considering the vast size of the market and the general resistance to change by its participants.

3.2 Definition and Types of Tokens

According to Baum (2020, p. 3), tokenization in the real estate technology world currently refers to one of the two things: fractionalization of property rights or digital representation of asset ownership. The MIT Digital Currency Initiative (Smith et al., 2019, p. 7) defines tokenization as the digital representation of an asset, based on blockchain technology. From these two definitions, the following can be deduced: the application of tokenization in real estate through the fractionalization of an asset usually also includes the digital representation of that asset first, but not the other way around. This means, there are other potential applications for blockchain and digital asset representation within the real estate industry which do not include fractionalization. However, when speaking about tokenization in real estate, fractionalization of an asset is often implied.

Consequently, a further distinguishment needs to be added to the definition of tokenization. As stated, the above definitions indicate the direct tokenization of a real estate asset. Meaning, that a token holder owns a share of the real estate asset and has a right to their proportional share of the return generated by that asset. However, due to various regulatory issues, which will be discussed in more detail in Sects. 3.4 and 3.5, most jurisdictions do not allow for the direct tokenization of real estate assets. Instead, an intermediate structure such as a special purpose vehicle (SPV) is established to hold the asset and is then tokenized. A token holder then owns a share of the SPV and is entitled to their proportional share of the return generated by the SPV. Consequently, the above definitions should, for the time being, be interpreted in a broader sense to include the tokenization of intermediate structures and participation rights (Liu et al., 2020, p. 20; de la Rubia et al., 2021, p. 6).

Multiple types of tokens have been created with blockchain technology. The payment token is probably the most known, as it is used for cryptocurrencies. Asset tokens and utility tokens are often brought into context with real estate. Together they can form a hybrid token. As described in Sect. 2.5 there are also other types of tokens with a range of different characteristics, however, for this paper, the focus will lie on these four. They are defined below (Lai et al., 2020, p. 6):

Payment/Exchange Token: A payment token such as Bitcoin aims to fulfil the functions of money—a medium of exchange, a store of value, and a unit of account.

While all cryptocurrencies could fulfil the first function, none has managed to fulfil all of them (Dr. Ammous, 2016).

Asset/Security Token: An asset token is the digital representation of ownership of a specific asset. It is directly tied to that asset and its value fluctuates with the value of the asset. Asset tokens can be distributed through an STO, a security token offering (Deloitte, 2021, p. 28).

Utility Token: A utility token gives the holder access to a product or a service. For example, the right to access and use a community building.

Hybrid Token: A hybrid token combines the functions of more than one type of token. In real estate, a hybrid token could, for example, simultaneously represent the ownership of a condominium and the right to use communal spaces in the same block (Baum, 2020, p. 34). Overall, tokens are flexible in design and customizable. They can contain a combination of different assets and rights (Deloitte, 2021, p. 28).

In addition to distinguishing between different types of tokens, there are also *fungible* and *non-fungible tokens*. Fungible tokens are interchangeable, meaning each token holds the same value. Just as one Bitcoin is always the same as another Bitcoin or a token representing one ounce of gold is interchangeable with another. Non-fungible tokens (NFTs), however, are not interchangeable. Each NFT is unique and valued individually (Lai et al., 2020, p. 7). Currently, NFTs are often associated with the digital representation of ownership and authenticity of, for example, a piece of art. In the context of real estate, an NFT could also be used to digitally represent the ownership of a property (in its entirety). This could facilitate the transaction process in the event of a change of ownership, which often requires a lot of due diligence, administrative paperwork, and therefore time (Sonenreich, 2022). When fractionalizing and tokenizing a real estate asset directly, the issued tokens would be considered fungible tokens as each token would represent an equal share of the underlying security.

3.3 Opportunities and Applications

Academic research (Nijland & Veuger, 2019, p. 22; Baum, 2020, p. 4) as well as market reports (Liu et al., 2020, p. 7; Pang et al., 2020, p. 6) agree that the real estate asset class is traditionally illiquid, inaccessible and lacks transparency. Illiquid, because of the highly manual and time-consuming administrative processes which are required for a transaction and because most transactions are carried out in private markets, omitting a large pool of potential investors. A traditional real estate transaction also requires intermediaries, which in turn increases costs. As a result of these factors, real estate is often considered lumpy. It is inaccessible, because of the high capital requirements, and because transactions are carried out privately and on an irregular basis. The lack of transparency is another classic drawback of the traditional real estate investment market. Information around a property is often incomplete and kept privately, there is no central database. Intermediaries and thorough due diligence are therefore required to verify all the data, making the process more time and cost intensive. Finally, inaccuracies, human error, and fraud are also considered common concerns.

Non-qualified investors or non-accredited investors in the USA—retail investors—can rarely directly invest in real estate outside of purchasing their own home, which is already considered a privilege by many. At the same time, alternative investments receive a lot of attention and increased asset allocation. Real estate in particular is considered one of the top three alternative asset classes for institutional investors and is generally seen as a good inflation hedge and diversifier in an investment portfolio by having a low correlation to stock indices (Lai et al., 2020, pp. 13–14). However, only a few investors can take advantage of this vast asset class and the profitable returns it generates.

Real estate mutual funds or real estate investment trusts (REITs), for example, currently already allow for the investment in fractionalized real estate with little capital. However, unlisted funds (open- or closed-ended) can require a considerable minimum investment. While for the fund manager, the process of raising capital sometimes still comes down to convincing investors one and by one and generally includes very little automation. Here, a more efficient primary market distribution platform and liquid secondary market are called for (Baum, 2020, p. 13). Also, the fund manager, or in the case of an REIT, the investment manager decides on the investment strategy and chooses the assets to be bought. Little individualization is possible by the investor. Additionally, funds and REITs mostly take a fee in exchange for their services (Liu et al., 2020, p. 21). Apart from real estate mutual funds and REITS, other funds (not focused solely on real estate), exchange-traded funds (ETFs), or private equity companies, for example, invest in real estate (directly or indirectly).

Another way to invest in fractionalized real estate is through crowdfunding. Crowdfunding is an alternative to traditional capital raising, applying some of the strategic advantages of tokenization. In crowdfunding the minimum investment amount is usually low, widening the potential pool of investors. Crowdfunding is also carried out via a digital platform and does not require an intermediary agent. Digital distribution, furthermore, could allow for investments to take place across borders. Similarly, there are other platforms that allow for peer-to-peer lending or debt crowdfunding for mortgages as well (Baum, 2020, p. 10).

3.3.1 Potential Benefits

Tokenization represents an alternative sphere to the traditional real estate market and current real estate investment opportunities with the potential to overcome many of the common shortcomings. In the primary market, the fractionalization of assets could increase demand, draw more international attention, and simplify the process of raising capital. Reinforced through decentralization, the application of smart contracts and blockchain-based ownership records, the secondary market could be strengthened through increased transparency, liquidity, and efficiency (Baum, 2020, p. 9).

The largest drivers for these improvements are manifold and agreed upon by first movers in the market such as Pang et al. (2020, p. 7) and Laurent et al. (2018), p. 63), academics such as Baum (2020, p. 32) and Smith et al. (2019, pp. 2, 11, 37), and local legal experts such as Dr. Catrina Luchsinger (2021):

- *Fractionalization*: Increasing the pool of potential investors by reducing the capital requirements and minimum investment periods, therefore, lowering the barrier to entry. It allows direct investment access for smaller investors, democratizing access to real estate assets.
- *Access to Capital*: Fractionalization, tokenization, and the digital distribution of said tokens can increase the pool of potential investors by many smaller-scale investors, possibly even on an international level. This can facilitate the process of raising capital and offer an alternative to traditional debt sources for private investors looking to, for example, purchase a home as it simplifies crowdfunding, as well as for professional investors and increase the success of STOs.
- *Liquidity*: The availability of much smaller shares of real estate and the resulting increase in the number of potential investors (assuming there is a digital distribution platform and secondary market exchange) can increase the liquidity of the asset itself—possibly even on an international level. Increased liquidity can make for a more attractive and potentially higher valued asset where owners benefit from a liquidity premium. It further increases the flexibility and adaptiveness of investors as transactions could be settled much quicker.
- *Customizability*: Direct real estate investment with small capital requirements allows investors to put together their very own, customized real estate investment portfolio. An element that is becoming increasingly more important as investment requirements have moved away from solely focusing on return (e.g., ESG). Also, as capital requirements significantly decrease, tokenization can further allow for increased diversification within an investment portfolio.
- *Transparency*: Due diligence and recordkeeping around, for example, chain-of-title, past renovations, or other underlying drivers of the value of the property can be facilitated through the implementation of blockchain. This increases data transparency and in turn security as it offers a single source of truth.
- *Automation*: The implementation of blockchain technology and smart contracts can automate certain steps, for instance, the payment of dividends, and, as a result, reduce administrative efforts, the involvement of intermediaries, and costs. Automated steps are, furthermore, less prone to human error.
- *Cost Reduction*: Automation, increased transparency, quicker access to capital, increased liquidity, decentralization, and the potential elimination of certain intermediaries all allow for cost reductions in real estate investment and real estate transactions.
- *Efficiency*: All the above-mentioned drivers in turn increase the efficiency of real estate investments and real estate transactions.

Additional benefits can be achieved through the application of blockchain and tokenization in real estate:

- *Synergies*: Synergies can be created through other additional applications of blockchain within the real estate industry, in property management, for instance.
- *Hybrid Tokens*: Hybrid tokens allow for even further customization of the token itself, where it does not only represent ownership but also the right to access a product or service.
- *Structured Products*: Tokenized assets will allow for the creation of additional financial products such as derivatives and, therefore, also for further value creation.
- *Optimize Portfolios*: Tokenized real estate assets could present a vast new investment opportunity and, as a result, impact portfolio construction and potentially even better risk-return profiles (Lai et al., 2020, p. 57).
- *Shared Ownership*: The option of only purchasing a share of a property could also increase the appeal of shared ownership. Friends or family could come together and purchase, for instance, a vacation home together. Blockchain technology and smart contracts could mediate and prevent many of the disagreements or difficulties which are otherwise quick to arise in such an arrangement (Stefanoski et al., 2020).

Considering the extensive list above, the potential of tokenization in real estate is apparent and worth pursuing further. Coming back to the alternatives of investing in fractionalized real estate today, comparisons have been made (Liu et al., 2020, p. 21; Lai et al., 2020, p. 43). REITs are generally considered the most accessible fractionalized real estate investment opportunity today. A comparison between REIT funds and real estate tokens can be seen in Figure 3.1. The comparison shows

	REIT Funds	Tokenisation
Fractionalisation	Limited variety and fixed proportions	Digitalisation enables fractionalisation to customise portfolio exposure
Operational Efficiency	Long, reptitive processes; siloed data; long settlement time	Digitalisation enables quicker settlement subject to the blockchain; smart contracts can automate processes
Settlement Time	Investor redemption request to receiving money around T+2/3	Digitalisation with digital ROM can be instantly updated
Data Transparency	Low data transparency (esp. unlisted REITs)	Blockchain brings data transparency, immutability and accessibility
Flexibility	No flexibility to balance exposure, limited to REIT exposure	Digitalisation enables fractional exposure traded within a managed or customised portfolio
Liquidity	Limited to shares	Digitalisation enables single assets, funds and unlisted REITs to be traded

Fig. 3.1 *REIT Funds* Vs. *Tokenization. Note.* From Lai et al. (2020), p. 43 (https://caia.org/tokenisation)

the customizability that tokenization permits, the efficiency which can be achieved through digitalization and smart contracts, the transparency, immutability, and decentralized accessibility of blockchain technology, and finally the increased liquidity of real estate tokens compared to REITs. While these are the potential benefits, comparisons between REITs and current use cases of real estate tokens don't show a difference between the two apart from the digitalization benefits (Liu et al., 2020, p. 21).

3.3.2 *Potential Applications*

Considering the vast potential benefits of tokenized and fractionalized real estate assets, the potential concrete applications are reviewed next. To do so, a framework by Graglia and Mellon (2018, p. 98) which was presented by Liu et al. (2020, pp. 24, 26–27) as part of their detailed analysis of the potential of DLT in real estate serves as a foundation and can be seen in Fig. 3.2. It starts at level 0, which is no integration of blockchain whatsoever. At level 1, blockchain is simply used to record documents. This can be valuable for real estate valuations in jurisdictions where there is no notary available or for real estate valuations. While the valuation itself would be carried out using the same standards and methods, the valuators would upload their reports to the distributed ledger instead of sending them directly to the client (e.g., a bank). The client can then access the reports by using the hash value. If the valuation is approved by the client, the information can be shared among all nodes in the network. A valuation would then only need to be carried out and uploaded once, decreasing the overall administrative efforts of the respective real estate market. Also, the other nodes in the network could verify key property data and the validity

Level	Name	Description
0	No integration	No use of blockchain
1	Blockchain recording	Public blockchain used to record documents related to land registration
2	Smart work-flow	Blockchain used to record progress of a transaction
3	Smart escrow	Smart contracts used for escrowing payment
4	Blockchain registry	Central database replaced with a permissioned block-chain
5	Disaggregated rights	Various rights to a single parcel are disaggregated and managed via blockchain
6	Fractional rights	Rights for a given parcel are fragmented and managed via blockchain
7	P2P transactions	Rights are transacted without intermediaries on level 4 system
8	Interoperability	Different blockchain registries merge

Fig. 3.2 *Blockchain in real estate: Levels of Integration. Note.* From Liu et al. (2020), p. 27. Liu et al. adapted the table from 'Blockchain and property in 2018: At the end of the beginning' by Graglia and Mellon (2018), p. 98. https://www.rics.org/globalassets/rics-website/media/knowledge/research/research-reports/rics0077-001-distributed-ledger-technology-review-report%2D%2Dfinal.pdf

of the valuation. A further potential application at this level lies in blockchain-based listing platforms, to increase the efficiency of property searches. The notion is based on the benefits which a peer-to-peer decentralized platform could offer compared to the often fragmented and incomplete listing platforms present today.

At level 2, the conveyancing of a property can be carried out digitally. The blockchain can speed up the process and increase transparency. It connects all required parties in one system, where seller and buyer(s) have to identify themselves and due diligence is only carried out once and can, once verified, be accessed by everyone in the network. Level 3 goes one step further and allows for the automatic completion (transfer of ownership and payment) of the transaction once all pre-determined conditions are met. Level 4 describes an on-chain land register. Starting at level 5 there are no recorded use cases. At level 5, other rights, apart from ownership and occupancy, are discussed. Such rights, for example, air rights, are separated from the property and traded on the blockchain. Level 6 represents true direct fractionalization of real estate rights, the basis of tokenization. Level 7 describes peer-to-peer transactions of such fractionalized real estate rights. Finally, level 8 illustrates a scenario in which the blockchains of various countries and jurisdictions work together, enabling peer-to-peer transactions of fractionalized real estate across different blockchains, creating a potentially global infrastructure. Naturally, this scenario entails challenges on a technical level, mostly in the form of defining standards, and more significantly on a political and regulatory level (Liu et al., 2020, p. 27).

Considering the potential integration of blockchain in the real estate market, there is, in theory, a range of possible applications for tokenization in the field of real estate. Institutional investors and asset managers are mostly looking to raise (more) capital through the broadened investor base or take advantage of the increased liquidity created through fractionalization and tokenization. Many papers and reports focus on the tokenization of a single real estate asset and the benefits it could offer. However, one could also consider tokenizing an entire portfolio, for example, or only tokenizing part of an asset (mostly less than 50% to avoid some of the regulatory challenges). This would allow for continued ownership while liquidating part of the asset(s). By freeing part of the invested capital, institutional owners could benefit from having increased capital for other investment opportunities (Don, interview, April 11, 2022—see Appendix C for transcript). Moreover, investors could benefit from not only tokenizing existing properties but also development projects. Again, the process of raising capital could be simplified. Furthermore, assuming there is a secondary market exchange, tokenization could also allow token holders (investors) to exit the project before completion (Pang et al., 2020, p. 19).

In any case, the tokens need to be distributed to investors following the issuance as part of the tokenization process. Stefanoski et al. (2020, p. 35) compared the traditional initial public offering (IPO), an STO, and an initial coin offering (ICO), the latter is less relevant in the context of this research as it is used for cryptocurrencies. While their comparison references to STOs with any underlying asset, it can be applied to the case of a real estate asset as well. Following the comparison, it can be deduced that a range of companies can benefit from an STO, whereas only large and established companies can carry out an IPO. Digital distribution of the tokens could allow for a more global reach and increase the potential investor base. The digital distribution also allows for direct market access without the need for an intermediary, decreasing complexity and costs. All in all, the comparison shows the potential tokenization holds in terms of fundraising compared to the traditional real estate market. Potential, which other reports have recognized as well (Liu et al., 2020, p. 20). Naturally, the current regulatory uncertainties, as well as the trustworthiness of companies, need to be considered as well.

Another potential application is the tokenization of the economic benefits of a private equity real estate fund. Here, the GPs could free additional capital by tokenizing part of their own economic interest in the fund, while the LPs could exit the fund in advance should they need or wish to liquidate their investment ahead of time. This could increase flexibility and liquidity for any closed-end fund (Pang et al., 2020, p. 19). Further applications mentioned is an employee incentive programme that was set up in Hong Kong in 2019. A property developer decided to tokenize the holding company of one of their properties and award high-performing employees with tokens. Token holders could then benefit through capital appreciation. The employees could further trade the tokens between themselves, and the programme could be extended to multiple holding companies and multiple properties (Pang et al., 2020, p. 24).

Private individuals, on the other hand, could also profit from tokenization. When looking to purchase a home, individuals could choose to issue tokens as opposed to going to a bank for a mortgage. The investors would regularly be paid interest and could potentially benefit from an appreciation of the property (Graglia & Mellon, 2018, p. 102). Alternatively, a lease-to-own scheme could be set up. The downpayment presents a large financial strain for many and can often prevent the purchase of a home. By fractionalizing and tokenizing a property, the lease-to-own arrangement could offer individuals the opportunity to purchase their home in small increments, at their own pace, a couple of tokens at a time. The seller or real estate firm could meanwhile benefit from the income (rent) that the property generates (Pang et al., 2020, p. 24). These concepts can also be applied the other way around. Many homeowners have had to invest a large part of their equity to purchase their property. Fractionalizing their asset and issuing tokens could free some of that capital for other projects (Yousuf, interview, April 6, 2022—see Appendix E for transcript). Finally, non-professional investors could, of course, benefit from the added investment opportunities which fractionalization and tokenization can bring to the market (Laurent et al., 2018, p. 64).

Overall, one should also consider the potentially major shift in power that the token economy represents. In many regions, the real estate industry is dominated by large, mostly institutional, investors. These investors enjoy a comparably large influence on the market and have been profiting well for a long time. A shift towards many smaller investors might, therefore, not be in everyone's interest. A shift towards fractionalized and tokenized real estate investments can, however, also present an opportunity if market participants succeed in adapting their business model to be a part of the tokenization value chain. There are multiple ways to do so, for example, offer consultancy on the topic, or build a cybersecurity service. Market participants who currently offer traditional services within the industry and fail to adapt their business model might find their competitive advantage suffering down the line (Laurent et al., 2018, p. 66).

3.3.3 Implementation

Having reviewed the potential benefits of tokenizing real estate as well as the potential areas of application, the question remains what the implementation process specifically looks like, and how does it work from a technological standpoint? Figure 3.3 below by Pang et al. (2020, pp. 8–19) shows the typical steps of a real estate tokenization process. DigiShares (2022, p. 5) has also illustrated the tokenization process, and so has EY (Stefanoski et al., 2020, pp. 20–21). The process below includes the steps and captions as established by Pang et al. but includes details as described by the other market participants as well.

1. *Deal Structuring*: To start the process, the issuers (owners or management) need to decide on some specifics. To do so, they should first reflect on their business objectives and the benefits they aim to create through tokenization, is it to increase liquidity, or to better raise capital? Only then can the issuers consider:

   - Which jurisdiction(s) will be relevant for the product, and the different regulations (accounting, reporting, KYC, AML, etc.) and tax implications that come with it.
   - What intermediate structure will work best for the specific project.
   - What will be tokenized; equity, debt, or a participation right/economic interest.
   - What the fee structure will look like as well as the number of tokens to be issued and the price of a token.
   - What rights and obligations investors will hold, and whether they will receive a return and/or benefit from the asset's potential appreciation.

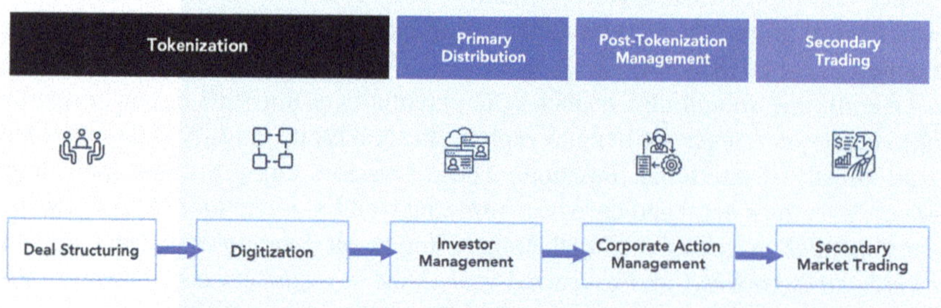

Fig. 3.3 *Lifecycle of a Tokenized Real Estate Asset. Note.* From Pang et al. (2020), p. 8 (https://www.colliers.com/en-hk/research/real-estate-tokenization)

2. *Digitization*: The digitization phase consists of setting up the blockchain, and coding and adding the necessary smart contracts. This includes various steps such as choosing and implementing a blockchain protocol, token standard (e.g., the ERC-1400 standard), custody solution and/or provider, automated compliance protocols, and so on. To decide on these fundamentals, a couple of aspects should again be considered, such as regulatory/legal constraints (which could, e.g., impact data privacy and protection), scalability requirements, and what specific functions might need to be added to be in line with the business process and concept. Once complete, it is, furthermore, recommended to have a third-party expert perform a security review before going live. The Ethereum blockchain is currently the most used technological standard for tokenization in real estate, followed by Stellar and Tezos (de la Rubia et al., 2021, p. 14). The ERC-1400 standard has meanwhile been the frontrunner for security tokens. Finally, a distribution plan should be developed and suitable payment method(s) chosen before the tokens can be issued and then distributed in the next phase.
3. *Investor Management*: The primary distribution of the tokens or STO can then be initiated. Tokens are usually sold in exchange for capital, which is often paid in the form of a cryptocurrency such as Ether (ETH) or a stable coin. The distribution can be handled on a digital channel and does not require an intermediary. Access to the issued tokens by investors is generally only limited by regulatory constraints (there should not be any technical constraints). Regulatory compliance in the context of, for example, anti-money laundering (AML) or know your customer (KYC) regulations is ensured as investors are required to create a profile or offer some personal information (while maintaining their anonymity) which is then verified by smart contracts. Following the distribution, the investors' data is uploaded onto the blockchain where a digital register of members (ROM) is created, serving as a record of ownership. The token holders, meanwhile, will store their token in a wallet for digital assets.
4. *Corporate Action Management*: Post-tokenization management includes automated processes such as dividend distribution and shareholder voting enabled by smart contracts. Also, accounting and reporting processes can be handled without the need for a third party and be automated and executed with smart contracts. Exposed functions, furthermore, allow token holders to interact with their token and, for example, initiate a transfer. In the case of a transfer, the change in ownership will first be checked for its regulatory compliance and then automatically recorded on the blockchain, immutably and transparent to all participants. Providers have also created tools for issuers to keep track of their blockchain and monitor changes, for instance, EY's Blockchain Analyzer.
5. *Secondary Market Trading*: Finally, a token holder can decide to liquidate their investment by selling their tokens to another investor. Currently, there is no secondary market exchange for tokens but ideally, secondary trading would take place on a peer-to-peer basis, as opposed to via established digital exchanges. The trading could be carried out without a central third party (for clearing and settlement) thanks to the underlying blockchain technology.

3.3.4 *Smart Contracts in Real Estate Tokenization*

One element which is thought to be crucial for the successful implementation of tokenization in real estate is smart contracts (Pang et al., 2020; Liu et al., 2020, p. 17; de la Rubia et al., 2021, p. 11). Many of the benefits of tokenization in real estate mentioned earlier are only made possible through the application of smart contracts. A smart programme does exactly as programmed. If certain requirements are fulfilled, it automatically takes the pre-determined action. In terms of real estate transactions, the advantages of smart contracts over a traditional intermediary are apparent and have been stated by market participants. First and foremost, experts see high potential in smart contracts being able to carry out transactions more efficiently. Smart contracts could, furthermore, increase trust as they are highly predictable and less prone to human error (Liu et al., 2020, p. 17).

Apart from transactions, smart contracts can also be beneficial in terms of property management. If a building has multiple, passive owners, the management of said building can become difficult. Or what happens if a tenant moves out, doesn't pay rent, or renovations are necessary, for example (Baum, 2020, p. 18)? Here, smart contracts come into play. They could, for example, be connected to sensors set up on the property which can automatically update the smart contract on, for example, damage following a storm (de la Rubia et al., 2021, p. 18). Further advantages can be created by, for example, having the smart contract check that rental agreements are signed correctly and on time (Liu et al., 2020, p. 17).

With such features, smart contracts can enable the creation of a decentralized autonomous organization (DAO). A DAO is organized among its owners in a decentral manner. Tokens represent the fractionalized ownership of each investor and smart contracts contain the terms of that ownership. Smart contracts further reflect the structure of the DAO, how it behaves, and how it can evolve. They are automated pre-defined rules and processes. Such a structure is also known as a decentralized autonomous space (DAS). A visualization of a DAO, or in the case of real estate a DAS, can be seen in Fig. 3.4. It also depicts the differences to traditional real estate management which are mainly based on the absence of an intermediary and two-way communication between owners/shareholders and the DAO as well as between contractors/suppliers and the DAO (Ceccon, 2021).

Smart contracts can also be used for additional tasks. This includes the automation of processes such as AML and KYC procedures, periodic reporting, and dividend payouts, which in turn optimizes both real estate management and investment and transaction processes. This can result in significant time and cost savings for all parties involved (Pang et al., 2020, p. 14). Finally, smart contracts allow for the creation of hybrid tokens. So, in addition to representing ownership, other rights can be given to a token holder. For example, if invested in a hotel, a token holder could be offered a free hotel night per year (Luchsinger, 2022, p. 4).

Overall and irrespective of the application of fractionalization and tokenization, the report by Liu et al. (2020, p. 19) showed that almost 60% of market participants expect wider adoption of smart contracts in the real estate market in the next five

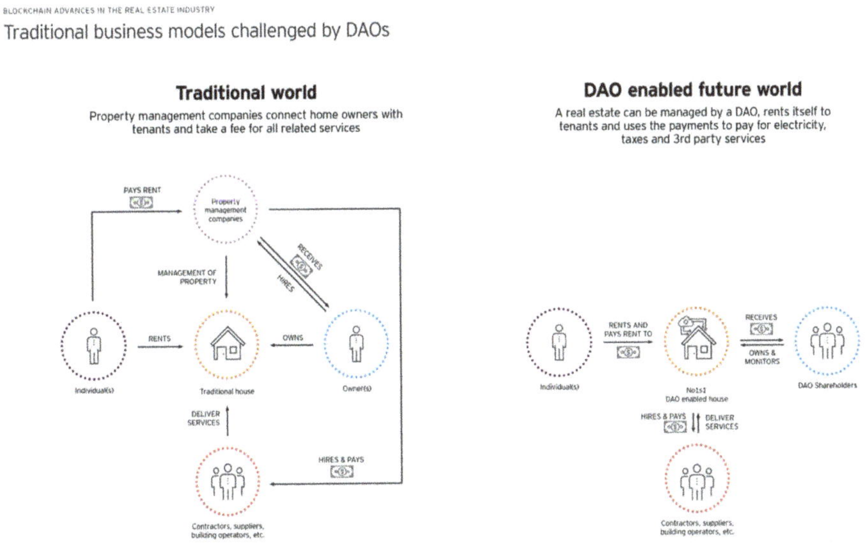

Fig. 3.4 *DAO in real estate. Note.* From 'What happens when buildings own and manage themselves?' by Ceccon (2021). https://www.ey.com/en_ch/strategy/what-happens-when-buildings-own-and-manage-themselves

years. However, the use of smart contracts is not necessarily as straightforward as expected. According to Luchsinger (2022, p. 4), smart contracts require a thorough knowledge of real estate management. When managing real estate, it is, for example, important to build a CapEx fund to finance larger renovations in the future. If such business practices are not included in the smart contract, challenges can arise along the way. Especially, as it is difficult to change a smart contract in retrospect (Stefanoski et al., 2020, p. 25). Furthermore, bugs in smart contracts have led to damaging results in the past and should therefore be reviewed carefully and implemented with caution (Monrat et al., 2019, p. 117148).

3.4 Challenges and Drawbacks

Considering the benefits established in Sect. 3.3, tokenization in the real estate market should have a promising future ahead and could potentially transform the entire industry. However, most elements are in the early development stages and there are still many challenges and uncertainties to overcome. These include tax, accounting, valuation, and regulatory challenges but also technical and political hurdles. The regulatory difficulties are often considered the biggest limitation for the wide adoption of tokenization in real estate, especially as there are strong regional differences (Baum, 2020, p. 3). This subchapter will highlight the main challenges.

3.4.1 Regulatory Framework

Regulatory constraints impact whether and how a real estate asset can be fractionalized and tokenized. It is currently not possible to incorporate ownership through tokens in land registers (Liu et al., 2020, p. 20). Even if that issue could be solved, changes in ownership still need to be recorded in the land register, which can be a lengthy and costly process (Luchsinger, 2022, p. 2). A functioning, liquid, and global secondary market exchange for trading real estate tokens, however, would require ownership changes to be registered within minutes, 24/7. Sull and Baum (2019, pp. 21–22), therefore, stated that the digitalization of land registers is the most urgent reform necessary. They further concluded that the development of the technology will outpace the market's capacity to implement it. Pang et al. (2020, p. 22) also pointed out that while the market expectancy is for jurisdictions to start to or continue to adapt to the new market developments and technological opportunities there is no guarantee for it. Not ensuring a safe regulatory framework, however, opens the door for scams or hackers. Should blockchain and tokenization be increasingly attributed to such criminal activities, it would be even more difficult to convince market participants of its many benefits (Laurent et al., 2018, p. 64).

To tackle these challenges, the use of an intermediate structure is often suggested (Baum, 2020, p.18; Luchsinger, 2021) and has already been applied, for example, by RealT in the USA using Inc. and LLC (RealT, n.d.). Baum (2020, p. 18) explained that there are four broad intermediate ownership forms available: a company, partnership, trust, and a KVG (*Kapitalverwaltungsgesellschaft*) in Germany. They, furthermore, concluded that they see the most potential in using a fund structure. Intermediate structures, however, can tear at the advantages of tokenization. Efficiency and cost reductions, for example, might not be achieved at the same level. Ultimately, advantages in efficiency, transparency, and liquidity need to outweigh possible costs, for market participants to move towards tokenization. Introducing tokenization in real estate using intermediate structures might be a good starting point though and can help familiarize the industry with these new technological opportunities (Baum, 2020, pp. 4, 55). There are additional, legal challenges to consider such as the requirement of a notary for a change in ownership or tax issues. More details on the legal basis and possibilities in Switzerland specifically are explained in Sect. 3.5.

3.4.2 Political Opposition

The potential political opposition should be considered as well. Opening the market to a broader investor base might increase real estate and land prices even further due to increased liquidity, a liquidity premium could be the result. This could, in turn, lead to opposition from the public and politicians (Dr. Luchsinger, 2022, p. 2). Furthermore, some investors currently take advantage of the illiquidity of the real estate market to make larger returns (Liu et al., 2020, p. 23).

Further opposition could come from market participants which might see their role in the real estate value chain diminish. A decentralized land register, secondary market exchange, and transactions carried out on blockchain could reduce and/or change the demand for certain professionals such as lawyers or brokers. Their reluctance to push a wider implementation of tokenization in real estate could be challenging (Liu et al., 2020, p. 16). However, some market participants have stated that a wider implementation is only a matter of time, and professionals which fail to adapt their services accordingly might struggle later on (Laurent et al., 2018, p. 67).

3.4.3 Technical Challenges

Even though many share the general view that the technical basis is available, and it is mainly regulations and market players which need to catch up, there are still some technical challenges to consider. Scalability is still a concern, for example. Currently, the number of transactions that can be processed by a public blockchain such as Ethereum is limited. Another technical concern is security. While blockchain technology is considered immutable and highly transparent, it is still not 100% safe. Naturally, however, the question arises whether any technology can ever be 100% safe from mal use. Finally, the interoperability between multiple blockchains and respective standards still needs to be discussed and established (Liu et al., 2020, pp. 11, 33).

3.4.4 Data Confidentiality

An additional element to consider is data transparency throughout a real estate transaction process. Increased transparency is usually mentioned as a potential benefit of using blockchain technology in real estate. Using blockchain can allow for quicker due diligence and increased trust in the data provided and between participants. However, that is often under the assumption of a private or semi-private transaction process. Issuing the tokens of a highly fractionalized asset to a broad investor base will require the presentation of sensitive property data in a very public manner (Pang et al., 2020, p. 22). This issue could be solved by using a private as opposed to a public blockchain. A private blockchain could, furthermore, be more scalable as its network is a lot smaller. However, a private blockchain is also more vulnerable to, for example, hacks. It is also more centralized than a public blockchain which might not be in line with the initial concept (Liu et al., 2020, p. 119).

3.4.5 Trust

One of the biggest selling points of DLT solutions is that they can offer a peer-to-peer platform that does not require an intermediary for trust. However, blockchain technology, for a retail investor, does still require trust. Trust in the underlying cryptography, in the blockchain protocol, and in the smart contracts. While the protocol and coding can be viewed by anyone, many might not have the technical knowledge to truly understand them (Liu et al., 2020, p. 11; de la Rubia et al., 2021, p. 10). Here, a third-party review could come into play (Stefanoski et al., 2020, p. 26) or the readability of codes could be improved (Zheng et al., 2020, pp. 4–6).

Trust is also required in the case of a private blockchain, which is less decentralized and partly controlled by its operators. It further comes into play when considering the quality of, for example, property data that is put onto a blockchain. It could be difficult for the network to identify subpar data (Liu et al., 2020, pp. 11, 15). Market participants have therefore questioned whether blockchain technology can solve the 'garbage in, garbage out' problem (Lai et al., 2020, p. 10).

3.4.6 Demand

It is not yet evident whether there truly is a demand for fractionalized real estate assets. Are private investors interested in purchasing a small share of real estate? As a result of this uncertainty, Baum (2020, p. 4) stated their concern that the implementation of tokenization in the real estate industry could be set back by years, should development solely focus on the fractionalization of individual assets, and then not be deemed successful. This would add to the already present uncertainty around blockchain and tokenization in real estate by market participants.

Liu et al. (2020, p. 22) also analysed the demand for tokenized real estate investment opportunities and established four criteria that need to be met for wider adoption to take place: 'a lack of trust, the need to share data, the existence of a transaction, and that all parties in the network must benefit'. They concluded that a lack of trust could be an issue in markets where REITs or other alternative fractionalized real estate investment opportunities are not yet established. While transactions are taking place in the market for tokenized real estate, it is unclear whether there is a need to share data. Data transparency requirements are lower for tokenized real estate compared to REITs or other real estate funds. Finally, while both issuers and investors could benefit from tokenized real estate investments it is still unclear whether all benefits can be realized, as already established.

3.4.7 Lack of Education and Understanding

The lack of demand could stem from a lack of education, understanding of, and trust in tokenization and generally the underlying blockchain technology. There is a clear need for familiarizing the market and its retail investors with blockchain technology, smart contracts, and tokens to increase awareness and trust. They form the basis for understanding the true potential of tokenization, which is key for pushing development and demand. Education is also important in terms of risks. Investors need to understand that there are potential risks of investing in real estate tokens and what these look like, just as with any other investment (Lai et al., 2020, p. 59; Liu et al., 2020, pp. 7–8).

3.4.8 Secondary Market Exchange (or Lack Thereof)

Another limitation slowing down the broad implementation of tokenization is the missing exit strategies (Luchsinger, 2022, p. 4). Even if real estate assets are known to be held by investors for decades, they want to know that there are ways to liquidate their assets should they require to. Improving the illiquidity of real estate is one of the key promises tokenization holds. However, it will only be able to deliver on this promise with a functioning secondary market exchange. Currently, tokens are mostly traded on the issuers' own platforms, creating a highly fragmented market (Liu et al., 2020, p. 22). As long as a central secondary market exchange is still missing, investors will be hesitant about buying tokens in the first place, especially if there are lock-up periods for their initial investment.

In conclusion, most experts and market players agree that a communal effort will be necessary to further push the development of tokenization in real estate and enable wider adoption. Governments, (central) banks, and private companies will need to work together to build a working and interoperable infrastructure and ecosystem around blockchain and tokenization, harvesting the full potential that tokenization holds while also protecting investors, particularly new retail investors. This entails for competitors to work together, which could pose a further challenge. For a broad application, digital identification of buildings, so a form of digital land register, a legal system, and governmental guidance are seen as essential (Lai et al., 2020, p. 59; Laurent et al., 2018, p. 66; Pang et al., 2020, p. 25; Liu et al., 2020, pp. 7-8). However, as these requirements are hard to fulfil, even in well-developed jurisdictions, emerging countries might be the early adopters of these new technical solutions (Liu et al., 2020, p. 32).

3.4.9 Legal Foundation in Switzerland

The previous chapter on the current challenges for tokenizing real estate showed that regulatory matters are one of the largest concerns. A more detailed evaluation of the topic is essential to provide a more complete representation of the current state as well as the potential future developments in the field. Specifically, this sub-chapter summarizes the Swiss legal foundations surrounding the ownership of real estate and transfer of ownership. The changes following the complete coming into force of the DLT Act in 2021 (The Federal Council, 2021) are then reviewed, and as direct co-ownership is not yet a possibility in Switzerland (Dr. Luchsinger, 2021), the different alternatives to structuring and tokenizing indirect real estate investments are presented. Finally, the taxation of tokens in Switzerland is analysed. To further deepen the understanding of the topic, an interview with financial market and corporate law as well as token expert Dr. Catrina Luchsinger was carried out. A summary of the interview can be found at the end of the chapter and the transcript of the interview can be found in Appendix B. The summary focuses on reflecting on the key points of the interview.

As established in the previous chapter, Switzerland can be considered a hub for companies looking to drive the tokenization of real estate. There are multiple reasons for this. Switzerland has, historically, been known for its banking and financial infrastructure. Coupled with a highly educated workforce, favourable tax and regulatory environment, political stability, and international neutrality, it lends itself well as a base for fintech companies (Stefanoski et al., 2020). It is, therefore, important to review and analyse what specific elements in the regulatory and tax environment are currently advantageous for the continued development of the token economy and what pieces are still missing or need adapting.

3.4.10 Land Register and Cadastre

The real estate market in Switzerland functions on top of a detailed but often slow administrative structure. The main elements of this structure are the public land register and cadastral system—together they ensure safe land ownership in Switzerland (swisstopo, 2017). At its core, the land register is an official record of plot ownership. While the federal government is the supervisory authority for the land register, it falls under the jurisdiction of the respective cantons to establish appropriate land registry offices. Each entry in the land register corresponds to a plot of land and is allocated a specific parcel number. The entry, furthermore, encompasses the owner(s), details on notices (*Anmerkungen*) and priority notices (*Vormerkungen*), easements (*Dienstbarkeiten*), and encumbrances/liens (*Grundpfandrecht*) (cadastre.ch, a). The cadastral system and surveying, on the other hand, most importantly, collects and updates data on the plots of land. Again, the federal government represents the supervisory authority, namely the Federal

Office of Topography. The surveying and collection of data, however, is carried out on a cantonal and municipal level (cadastre.ch, b). The main data incorporated into the Swiss cadastre are property boundaries. Additionally, a range of other geographic data such as the buildings on the plots and border points are included (swisstopo, 2017).

When a real estate investment and, as a result, a transfer of ownership take place, the land register, by law (ZGB, Art. 656), needs to be changed. When applying to add or adapt an entry in the land register, the respective registry often charges a fee. Additionally, it can take months for the changes to be made (Dr. Luchsinger, 2022). An immediate entry into the journal (*Tagebuch*) of said application, however, is required (ZGB, Art. 948). Furthermore, the transfer of ownership of immovable property, here a plot of land, requires a public deed (*öffentliche Beurkundung*) (OR, Art. 216). For a public deed, an authorized public or private notary is required. The notary makes sure the respective parties are present or validly represented, and that all parties have included and understood the key elements of the written contract.

These are the very basic legal foundations that need to be taken into account when discussing real estate investment and transactions in Switzerland. For real estate tokenization to work on a large, nationwide scale, this structure and these laws will need to either be complied with or changed. Both alternatives come with challenges. Respecting and adapting to current laws mean dealing with intermediaries such as the registry or a notary. This adds to the complexity of the transaction, can result in a time lag between the signing and closing of a deal, and accrue additional costs. Changing the law or structure, on the other hand, could prove to be a very difficult and lengthy process.

3.4.11 DLT Act

Meanwhile, the Swiss judiciary has taken steps in the right direction with the approval and coming into force of the DLT Act in 2021. The DLT Act adapted ten federal laws in the Swiss Code of Obligations (*Obligationenrecht, OR*), the Federal Intermediate Securities Act (*Bucheffektengesetz, BEG*), and the Federal Act on International Private Law (*Bundesgesetz über das Internationale Privatrecht, IPRG*). (The Federal Council, 2021). These changes further increase the legal security around digital securities and strengthen Switzerland as a leading location for blockchain and token development (PwC, 2022b).

Most importantly, the act introduced a new form of uncertificated security and allows for the issuing of licences for DLT trading facilities. Such securities are to be registered within a DLT protocol. This new form of security has the advantage that it can be transferred and executed on the protocol without requiring further approval. It is expected to facilitate the issuing of DLT securities for companies looking to raise capital. DLT securities are also expected to be more liquid as the DLT trading facilities will allow for the multilateral trading of the securities and, also, allow direct access to private individuals. Different from traditional trading facilities, DLT trading facilities may also offer custody, clearing, and settlement services, allowing for the trade to be carried out on a blockchain with the help of smart contracts, requiring fewer intermediaries and time. The licensing of DLT trading facilities is regulated by the Swiss Financial Market Supervisory Authority (FINMA) (FINMA, n.d.) and follows similar requirements to traditional trading facilities, including having to be operated by a Swiss entity (an entirely decentralized exchange is, therefore, not yet possible) (PwC, 2022a). Additional to the issuing of licences for DLT trading facilities, the act includes provisions that were made to better legal certainty in the case of bankruptcy, allowing for the segregation of digital securities. Also, several other laws had to be adapted and extended as a result, for example, the extension of the Anti-Money Laundering Act (AMLA) to apply to DLT trading facilities as it will be considered a financial intermediary (The Federal Council, 2021).

In addition to having increased legal security regarding digital securities, there are still matters which are unclear. In such cases, there is the option to compose a non-action letter to FINMA, presenting the issue and suggesting a solution. FINMA will review the letter and either agree or disagree with the proposed solution. While this might be a lengthy process it provides added legal security in the market (Dr. Luchsinger, interview, May 4, 2022—see Appendix B for transcript).

3.4.12 Legal Structures

In general, the legal foundations to be considered when tokenizing real estate depends on the chosen legal structure of the intermediate ownership entity, the location of the underlying real estate asset, and the type of investors. These elements determine which jurisdictions and which regulations apply. Currently, it is not (yet) possible to register direct co-ownership in the Swiss land register. For this to be the case, the land register would ideally need to be on a blockchain as well. As a result, the direct tokenization of real estate assets in Switzerland is not possible. To bypass this difficulty, a range of different intermediate legal structures can be used to enable the creation of tokenized indirect real estate investments. Each structure comes with its advantages and disadvantages and there is not necessarily one correct form for everyone. The choice depends on the prerequisites of the issuers, their business model, and what they are comfortable with. The most common models are described below (Dr. Luchsinger, interview, May 4, 2022):

- *Real estate fund (Immobilienfonds)*: A Swiss fund needs a registered head office in Switzerland. A fund must be authorized and regulated by FINMA (time-consuming), and a pre- approved prospectus and key investor information document (KIID) are required. The invested funds need to be distributed between at least ten properties and can be leveraged by maximum 1/3. Shares can be distributed to qualified and non-qualified investors and investors generally hold a right of return.

- *Limited partnership for collective investment (Kommanditgesellschaft für kollektive Kapitalanlagen)*: This is a closed-end collective investment scheme regulated by FINMA (time-consuming), usually with a 7- to 9-year term. Shares can only be distributed to qualified investors and investors do not hold a right of return throughout the investment period. Few investment restrictions apply. A Swiss corporation acts as a general partner with unlimited liability, increasing flexibility compared to a fund.
- *Real estate company* (*Immobiliengesellschaft*): A real estate company is not subject to financial market supervision. It can be set up with a limited-term or open-ended. No investment restrictions apply but an investment policy statement needs to be respected, and a prospectus is also required. It is generally taxed as a corporation (*Kapitalgesellschaft*). When a token is resold, Swiss investors are exempt from taxation on capital gains. Also, retained earnings are taxed as part of the income of shareholders upon liquidation of the company. An exit can be difficult for investors without market making. It is generally, the easiest set-up; however, it is limited to qualified investors.
- A real estate company can also be set up for non-qualified investors. It then needs to be listed on a Swiss stock exchange, such as the newly approved SIX Digital Exchange (SDX) (SIX, 2021), to not be considered a collective investment scheme (and be subject to supervision by FINMA). However, this can be time-consuming.
- *Special purpose vehicle* (*Zweckgesellschaft*): An SPV can be set up to hold one specific real estate asset. As the vehicle only holds one asset it is not subject to financial market supervision and regulations are similar to that of a real estate company. However, setting up one vehicle per asset can be expensive and inefficient.

Having chosen a suitable legal structure, the next step is to decide what exactly should be tokenized as there are different possibilities to create (indirect) real estate tokens. These possibilities can roughly be categorized in tokenizing equity, debt, or an economic interest. When tokenizing equity, the entity holding the real estate asset issues shares or participation certificates in a tokenized form, giving token holders dividend rights. When tokenizing debt, bonds are issued and tokenized. These bonds can be perpetual or with a fixed term. If they are issued with a fixed term, the question of repayment at the end of the term arises, where will those funds come from? They can also be set up with a variable interest or with a fixed interest. If a variable interest is chosen, there is a risk that FINMA might consider the set-up to be similar to a collective investment scheme, which would then put the entity under financial market supervision and further regulations would apply, as described above. Instead of tokenizing equity or debt, economic interest or participation rights (usufruct) can be tokenized. Compared to tokenizing equity, the investment is based on a contractual relationship and the token holder does not own part of the entity as they would with a share. The token issuer is also not obliged to pay back the investment as is the case for debt. The token holder of a tokenized economic interest is entitled to their respective payments based on, for example, the income of the entity.

The three categories are analysed further in the next section on the taxation of tokens (Dr. Luchsinger, interview, May 4, 2022).

The above-described options represent the most basic models. However, there are further possibilities. For example, a derivative participation of token investors could be set up. For a derivative participation to work, a second SPV is created which is invested in the equity of the first SPV or holds certain rights to the asset of the first SPV. The profit or income generated by the second SPV can then be tokenized by, again, issuing shares, bonds, or participation rights. Furthermore, a structured product would be a possibility as well or a SICAV or SICAF. However, these are not commonly used legal structures (Dr. Luchsinger, interview, May 4, 2022).

When choosing a set-up, the aim and strategy of the business model should be considered first, as with any traditional real estate project. Is it a buy-and-hold situation or do you want to sell? Also, how can investors get out, what are their exit strategies? Without an exit strategy, many might not invest in the first place. Choosing a suitable economic model for a project is fundamental and can largely influence its success. Further regulatory obstacles should be addressed when choosing an intermediate structure. These include KYC and AML laws which apply to investment and fund companies. Also, if a fund structure is used, the property manager requires an asset manager licence. If the tokenization essentially replaces the need for a mortgage, all existing mortgages on the property need to be paid off first and laws regulating leverage need to be respected. The need for an exit strategy has been mentioned, one exit strategy could be found in a secondary market exchange. However, such an exchange can only be created by regulated financial institutions and Switzerland is not yet open to technical solutions as proposed by token issuers. The recently launched SDX does not fulfil many of the expectations of a blockchain-based, peer-to-peer digital securities exchange. Finally, Lex Koller needs to be considered as well, as it limits the investment of foreigners into Swiss residential real estate to funds or exchange-listed products (Dr. Luchsinger, 2021).

3.4.13 *Taxation of Tokens*

A further regulatory concern to address is the taxation of tokens. Switzerland is, in fact, one of the jurisdictions with the most detailed guidance on the taxation of digital securities providing the market with legal certainty and guidelines. From a global perspective, Switzerland is in the sixth place according to the PwC Annual global Crypto Tax report 2021. While most jurisdictions have solved the question of capital gains tax in the case of buying or selling crypto-assets (there is no capital gains tax on crypto-assets in Switzerland), many other aspects remain largely unsolved and changes are introduced continuously (PwC, 2022b).

In Switzerland, taxation generally depends on the type of token. Three different types of tokens are recognized: the asset, payment, and utility token (or a hybrid version). Tokens created within real estate will most likely be asset tokens. In a next step, three further categories are differentiated: investment token with a contractual basis, investment token with participation rights, and debt token. Taxation regulations are then based on the assumption that a Swiss corporation (*Aktiengesellschaft*, the most common form of *Kapitalgesellschaft*) holds the asset(s) (Eidgenössische Steuerverwaltung, n.d.).

Investment tokens with a contractual basis are issued for the purpose of collective fundraising. Token holders are entitled to a proportionate monetary payment proportionate either based on the issuer's EBIT or income, or on profit or liquidation proceeds. As such the investment is not considered to be equity (as no participation rights are distributed) or debt (as no bonds are distributed). The legal relationship between the investors and the token issuer is of contractual basis and the issuer is not obligated to repay the investment. The accrued funds qualify as taxable income on the side of the issuer (*Gewinnsteuer*), a contractual obligation to a specific project, however, can justify building reserves in the corresponding amount. The issuance of investment tokens with a contractual basis is further not subject to stamp tax (*Stempelabgaben*). Payments to investors qualify as a tax-deductible expense. The payments are also not subject to withholding tax (*Verrechnungssteuer*), provided that the shareholders of the corporation do not hold more than 50% of the tokens and payments do not exceed 50% of EBIT (safe harbour rules). From the investor's side, token earnings are also not subject to withholding tax, however, income tax (*Einkommenssteuer*) applies. The tokens themselves are subject to property tax (*Vermögenssteuer*). Finally, should a token be transferred to a different owner no transfer stamp tax applies.

An investment token with participation rights represents a share or participation certificate. The pro rata entitlement to profit is specified in the articles of association. The funds which are received as part of the issuance of the investment tokens are not subject to income tax on the issuer's side. The issuance is, nonetheless, subject to stamp tax. Also, payments are subject to withholding tax. From the investor's perspective, token earnings are likewise considered dividends and are subject to withholding payment tax and income tax. The token itself is, furthermore, subject to property tax. In the case of transaction and change in ownership, transfer stamp tax applies.

A debt token includes the obligation of the issuer to repay the investment and possibly the payment of interest. From the issuer's side, the accrued funds are considered a credit in the balance sheet and are not subject to income tax or issuance stamp tax. The payment of interest qualifies as a tax-deductible expense but is subject to withholding tax. From the investor's side, debt tokens are subject to property tax and dividends are subject to income tax and withholding tax. Capital gains resulting from the sale of a token are exempt from taxation, but a transfer stamp tax applies.

Finally, for all three categories of the asset token, the underlying asset has to be examined further to determine the correct VAT treatment. Also, as was established at the beginning of this section, these tax regulations are based on the assumption that the assets are held by a Swiss corporation. However, in the previous section, a range of different legal structures were presented. The choice of structure can impact taxation. Having said that, the explained models and regulations are often more complex in practice and need to be evaluated on a case-to-case basis. Should the direct tokenization of real estate assets become a possibility at some point, taxation would not necessarily be simplified. Issues such as the real estate gains tax would need to be addressed (PwC, 2022b).

3.4.14 Interview: Dr. Catrina Luchsinger

Dr. Catrina Luchsinger, a partner at MLL and token expert, was interviewed on April 4, 2022, in Zurich by the author of this paper. The interview transcript can be found in Appendix B. The interview with Dr. Luchsinger was critical for composing the above explanations on the current regulatory possibilities and limitations. The interview also discussed the interviewee's opinion on the current and future state of the (real estate) token industry in Switzerland and abroad.

Dr. Luchsinger describes the current blockchain and crypto infrastructure as highly fragmented. Many of the existing platforms are not interoperable and a multitude of wallets and exchanges are necessary to personally handle digital assets. In short, there is a lack of standards. Also, many of the user interfaces are not very user-friendly. Overall, people have a hard time understanding the technology, and many are worried about security. Still, the interviewee wants to encourage to start exploring and using the different available platforms.

When asked about the key elements which have put Switzerland at the forefront of token development Dr. Luchsinger referred to the existing regulatory framework and understanding of tokens. Regulatory security has been enabled through quick analysis and action by FINMA. Moreover, there are many highly knowledgeable consultants on matters of the law, tax, technology, and so on, which help the market in finding and applying suitable blockchain and token solutions. One of the more recent developments has been the launch of the SDX, an exchange platform for digital securities. Unfortunately, SDX is not the platform the market had hoped for. It does not truly enable peer-to-peer transactions of digital securities. Meanwhile, Japan has the goal to create a digital exchange for securities by the end of the year. This could truly be a game-changer: an approved, peer-to-peer network in a secure jurisdiction.

Regarding other competing countries, Dr. Luchsinger pointed out that real estate is a very market- specific field and international competition is not as much of a discussion. Still, Liechtenstein is well regulated, and in the Asian market, Singapore has developed well. The USA is by far the strongest in terms of tokenized financial products. In fact, some of these products couldn't be launched in Switzerland but are allowed to be distributed in Switzerland.

Naturally, the direct tokenization of real estate assets, which is currently not possible due to a range of limiting regulations, was discussed as well. Dr. Luchsinger believes that tokenizing real estate in such a manner will still take time. Multiple issues need to be addressed first. This includes Lex Koller, limiting the distribution of the tokens to foreign investors, as well as tax questions, for example, in regard to real estate gains tax. Meanwhile, their vision for the future is for new companies to choose to issue their shares as *Registerwertrechte*, which then can be tokenized. Furthermore, crypto banks will offer a (more centralized) solution to structure and organize the current infrastructure and address issues such as inheritance and secondary market exchanges. While setting up a secondary market will be hard for some assets, the digitization of data might still ease some of the administrative efforts, which already is a step in the right direction.

Ideally, Dr. Luchsinger wants to see a nationwide project to create a comprehensive connected digital data infrastructure using a permissioned blockchain. This blockchain would process and store most administrative data regarding, for example, plot ownership or car registrations, as well as hold personal data of all citizens such as their ID and health care information. Citizens and administrations should be able to simply log on to the blockchain and access their necessary data, increasing the efficiency and security of many administrative tasks. Having all this information on a blockchain would enable, amongst other things, the direct tokenization of real estate assets and could truly put Switzerland in a comfortable and stable position at the forefront of token development. People's trust in the government to carry out such a grand project in a secure manner is here. However, the creation of such an infrastructure will not happen in one big leap but in many small steps. The project could be started by creating an E-ID for all citizens, but development is slow. Some cantons are already working on implementing blockchain technology. Unfortunately, the cooperation between them is limited. If too many different blockchain standards are developed, the interoperability between the various cantons' blockchains will be hard.

3.5 Real Estate Token Market

Following the theoretical introduction to tokenization in real estate, this subchapter presents some of the current use cases, circumstances, and developments in the real estate token market to provide a more complete picture of the topic. This includes a global outlook as well as brief review of developments outside of the real estate industry.

3.5.1 A Global Perspective

According to a compilation by Dr. de la Rubia et al. (2021, p. 13), there were 41 companies tokenizing real estate by May 5, 2021. Out of the 41 companies 13 were based in the USA, 6 in Germany, and 3 in Switzerland. Out of the Swiss companies, two will be discussed in detail in Chap. 5, namely blockimmo and BrickMark. SwissRealCoin is a security token, where the underlying asset is a Swiss commercial real estate portfolio. SwissRealCoin is currently set on hold as future developments are being planned (SwissRealCoin, n.d.). When expanding the scope of analysis outside of Switzerland, several countries are also at the forefront of development in the real estate token market. Liechtenstein, Luxembourg, Germany, and the UK, for example, should all be considered. Outside of Europe the USA and Singapore are often mentioned. While these markets have not been analysed in detail some key elements will be highlighted next.

For Liechtenstein, their Tokens and Trustworthy Technologies Law (TVTG), which came into force on January 1, 2020, needs to be mentioned. The law is a collection of new rules and also includes changes to already existing laws. It allows for the tokenization of any right or asset according to the Token Container Model. This model shows how Liechtenstein differentiates between the underlying asset or right (which is in the container) and the token itself as a technical piece on the blockchain (the container itself). Liechtenstein was the first jurisdiction to establish a law for the token economy (Bitcoin Suisse, 2019). The company Crowdlitoken, which is also analysed in detail in Sect. 5.3, is based in Liechtenstein.

Meanwhile, Luxembourg further expanded its regulatory framework on January 28, 2021, allowing for the issuance of dematerialized securities with the use of DLT (Jacoby, 2021). More recently, on January 24, 2022, the Commission de Surveillance du Secteur Financier (CSSF) published a white paper on the topics of DLT and blockchain to guide market participants in the application of the technology in the financial sector, including advantages, risks, and adequate due diligence processes (CSSF, 2022). Digibrixx is a real estate tokenization company active in the real estate token market in Luxembourg. The company was established by Property Token and made compliant with the help of Tokeny (Tokeny, 2020). Digibrixx wants to enable anyone to invest in real estate projects in Luxembourg with as little as €500. Currently, investors can be a part of the Brahms Program, a project in Bertrange. Construction is supposed to be completed in March 2023 (Digibrixx, n.d.).

German legislation has also evolved. On June 10, 2021, a new law (Gesetz über elektronische Wertpapiere, eWpG) enabling the issuance of digital securities came into force. Instead of issuing securities with a physical certificate, securities can now be issued with an entry into the respective digital registry, either in a central registry or a registry for cryptocurrencies (Becker & Blassl, 2021). This law is part of the blockchain strategy by the federal government which was established in 2019 with the aim to take advantage of the technology and prevent misuse (Bundesministerium für Finanzen, n.d.). As mentioned above, Germany has seen a number of companies enter the real estate token market. Finexity, for example, is a platform allowing for the investment in a range of different tokenized asset-backed securities, including art, wine, cars, and real estate, creating access to illiquid assets (Finexity, n.d.). Meanwhile, Cashlink offers an all-in-one software solution for companies looking to tokenize securities, including the technological set-up and regulatory compliance (Cashlink, n.d.).

The UK is looking to become the future global cryptoasset technology hub according to the HM Treasury, where stablecoins would be a recognized form of payment. As part of this aim, a Cryptoasset Engagement Group has been established, the Royal Mint has been commissioned to create an NFT as an emblem of a future stablecoin, and the government is looking to create a more attractive tax environment for cryptoassets (HM Treasury, 2022). This course of action, however, is a big change from the past management of digital assets. The Financial Conduct Authority (FCA) has been very strict in admitting companies to their crypto register and has banned retail investors from trading crypto derivatives, in an attempt to prevent financial crimes. Market participants have been unhappy with the strict and often slow handling of things by the FCA, and they have been worried that the UK will fall behind in the development of blockchain applications and digital assets. It has, furthermore, caused businesses to set up abroad instead (Oliver & Stafford, 2022). It will be interesting to follow whether and how regulators in the UK will adjust to being more crypto-friendly. Still, the UK does have companies working within the field of tokenization in real estate. Bricktrade, for example, is a UK-based company offering investors to invest in UK real estate projects starting with £500. Meanwhile, developers have the opportunity to raise capital outside of the traditional lending market, assuming their project is approved by Bricktrade (Bricktrade, n.d.).

When analysing the European market, the proposed Markets in Crypto-Assets (MiCA) regulations must be mentioned as well. The regulations will be part of the EU's digital finance strategy, which aims to give consumers access to new and innovative financial products while also protecting them from misuse and ensuring overall financial stability (European Commission, 2020). MiCA is a legal framework for the EU's crypto-assets market, which aims to establish regulatory clarity on issues not yet covered by existing financial regulations while promoting further development and application of the technology but also ensuring consumer protection and financial stability. On March 14, 2022, the European Parliament adopted its stance on the regulations, changing the proposed legislative text and removing specific mentions of the proof-of-work consensus mechanism, which would otherwise have been prohibited due to its high energy consumption (Deloitte, 2022). While this change was gladly welcomed by the industry, reactions to the adjustments of AML and KYC regulations in early April were not as positive. While negotiations continue the MiCA is expected to be finalized at the end of the year and will then apply within the EU as of 2024 (Lee, 2022).

Having reviewed the European market, the USA is considered an important global player in the real estate token market. As mentioned in the beginning, most companies within the field have their base in the USA. The first-ever property to be tokenized was the St. Regis Aspen Resort in Colorado in 2018. AspenCoins were issued as a Securities and Exchange Commission (SEC) compliant regulated security and $18 million raised (Baum, 2020, p. 32). Following the successful tokenization of the St. Regis in Aspen, other companies followed. RealToken has tokenized a fair number of properties so far, or rather, they have tokenized a fair number of LLCs or Inc holding a real estate asset, mostly residential properties. For each property, a new token is issued and token holders receive their share of the profits (rent) on a weekly basis. Minimum investments range from $50-$150 depending on the property and tokens can be sold again on the RealToken platform (RealT, n.d.). In comparison, LABS currently only has hotel/resort projects in Indonesia and Singapore on their platform ready to invest in (LABS, n.d.). Meanwhile, MountX was the first company to tokenize properties in Mexico and is currently also offering investment opportunities in London (MountX, n.d.). RedSwan focuses mostly on commercial real estate in the USA, their range of properties is larger in comparison, with over 15 investment opportunities. Furthermore, they also have two funds, one is core and one is value-add, should an investor not wish to select a single property (RedSwan, n.d.). Finally, companies such as DigiShares and Harbor (Harbor, n.d.) offer tokenization services as opposed to investment opportunities.

In terms of regulation, there are large differences between the different states. While Wyoming, Colorado, and Ohio are very crypto-friendly and, for example, accept cryptocurrencies for tax payments, other states such as Iowa have prohibited this option. The issuance or trade of tokens is under the authority of the SEC and real estate-backed tokens will generally be considered a security and fall under the respective regulations (Dewey, 2022). Similar to the UK, President Biden issued an executive order (EO) on March 9, 2022, on 'Ensuring Responsible Development of Digital Assets'. In the EO, the President highlights the importance of protecting investors, financial inclusion of all citizens, ensuring (global) financial stability, and mitigating the misuse of the technology while still promoting further development to strengthen the US' position as a global financial leader and responsible innovator. Moreover, the EO places an urgency on researching and potentially developing a central bank digital currency (CBDC) (The White House, 2022).

Finally, the development in Singapore is briefly highlighted. Singapore has been considered to have an open but pragmatic approach towards blockchain and cryptoassets (Pereire & YingXin, n.d.). However, some market participants are worried about tightening regulations. On April 5, 2022, cryptocurrency regulations were extended to include business conducted across borders. The Financial Services and Markets Bill now requires providers of digital assets, who create the assets in Singapore but conduct business abroad to be licensed and adhere to AML and CFT (Combating the Financing of Terrorism) regulations. Providers operating in Singapore only are already regulated by the Monetary Authority of Singapore (MAS, the central bank) and adhere to licensing, AML, and CFT requirements (Loh, 2022). Fraxtor is a tokenization company based in Singapore. They currently offer investment opportunities for projects, funds, and bonds in Singapore, Australia, the UK, and Canada, and would therefore be affected by this change in regulations. Their projects are managed by private equity companies or real estate developers (Fraxtor, n.d.).

Naturally, the above-mentioned countries only represent a small selection. There are other countries that also have an open and positive attitude towards DLT and digital assets such as Australia, for example (Comply Advantage, n.d.). As of September 7, 2021, Bitcoin is even considered legal tender in El Salvador (Arslanian et al., 2021, p. 3). Meanwhile, Dubai adopted its first virtual asset law on March 9, 2022, to regulate cryptocurrencies and other digital assets. Simultaneously, the Dubai Virtual Assets Regulatory Authority (VARA) was established to oversee operations and trading activities (Business Insider India, 2022). In Japan, the Osaka

Digital Exchange (ODX) is expected to start handling trading activities as of 2023, creating Japan's first trading market for security tokens (Ledger Insights, 2021). It was established on April 1, 2021, and the majority of the shares are held by SBI PTS Holdings (70%) and Sumitomo Mitsui Financial Group (20%) (ODX Co. Ltd, n.d.). There are, however, also countries that have outright banned cryptocurrencies, China, Thailand, and Indonesia are among them (Loh, 2022).

Having done a brief analysis of what is happening around the world and in different jurisdictions, it is apparent that the market for blockchain applications, cryptocurrencies, digital securities, and tokens is not standing still. People have identified the potential within the technology and the possibilities it can create. As a result, market participants keep on innovating and establishing businesses, pressuring regulators for clarity, guidance, and support. From a political perspective, there is pressure to adapt and take advantage of these new possibilities and stay competitive on a global level. Furthermore, researching the different tokenization companies showed that the current market for real estate tokens is fractionalized. Also, the services and opportunities these companies offer differ from each other. While some companies offer investment opportunities on their platforms, such as RealToken and Crowdlitoken, other companies offer tokenization services such as Cashlink or Harbor. Overall, the token economy and infrastructure around real estate keep growing.

3.5.2 Developments and Applications Outside of Real Estate

Reviewing the developments and regulations around the globe also shows that real estate tokenization is only one of many potential blockchain applications and digital assets. Cryptocurrencies are clearly still at the forefront and many of the current discussions revolve around them. However, other digital assets such as the creation of NFTs for a variety of assets, or also the vast potential of metaverses (Prof. Dr. Dietrich, 2022) are gaining interest. Generally, any increased interest in blockchain applications and digital assets should be beneficial for the further understanding and development of real estate tokenization. Some recent happenings in the general space of blockchain applications and digital assets are, therefore, presented next, emphasizing the potential and relevance the topic has on a global level.

Apart from changing regulations and new providers in the market, the increasing interest in this new technology and its potential benefits and possibilities can also be observed for big established players. Generali Investments, for example, issued a press release on April 13, 2022, on the group's first transaction carried out on a blockchain. The transaction was completed by Generali Insurance Asset Management and €500,000 worth of bonds issued by the European Investment Bank (EIB) was purchased (Generali Investments, 2022). The issuance of the bond by EIB was led, amongst others, by Goldman Sachs (Goldman Sachs, 2021). In March 2022, the company further traded a Bitcoin non- deliverable option with Galaxy Digital, a crypto bank. The transaction represents the first over-the- counter

(OTC) crypto transaction by a major US bank (Galaxy Digital, 2022). More recently, Goldman Sachs invested in Elwood Technologies, a British cryptocurrency trading platform (Oliver, 2022).

Meanwhile, J.P. Morgan has established a Blockchain Centre of Excellence to research potential in- house applications of blockchain. As part of this organization, the JPM Coin was created in 2019 (Morgan, n.d.). While it has so far mostly served as a blockchain-based US dollar deposit account for corporate clients, the bank has been researching the programmability of the coin for conditional payments (Allison, 2021). In 2020, J.P. Morgan further established Onyx. Onyx is the first blockchain-based platform led by a bank. As part of this new business unit Liink was created, a blockchain network that enables peer-to-peer payment-related information exchanges. Onyx has recently worked with Siemens to develop a blockchain-based payment system for the German industrial group. The system automates payments between the company's accounts (Franklin, 2021). The adoption of the technology by banks can also be seen in HSBC and Wells Fargo agreeing to settle transactions by using blockchain (Szalay & Stafford, 2021).

The growing infrastructure and adoption of the technology can further be observed in companies such as EY or Deloitte, both international professional services companies. EY, for example, offers services covering the entire business lifecycle as they have created a range of different blockchain platforms (EY, n.d.). At the same time, Deloitte offers extensive consultancy on implementing blockchain solutions starting with identifying the right application area up until supporting the development of the blockchain (Deloitte, n.d.). Apart from established players, new companies have identified the potential of moving into the blockchain sphere. Sygnum, for example, received a lot of attention within the Swiss financial market. They say to be the world's first digital asset bank and specialist and use DLT to offer a range of solutions to their clients (Sygnum, n.d.). Finally, a review of further developments in the blockchain and digital assets space would not be complete without mentioning the newly launched SDX, an exchange platform for digital securities by SIX (SIX, 2021). While SIX is attempting to solve the issue of a missing secondary market exchange, the platform is not what some market participants had hoped for (Don, interview, April 11, 2022; Dr. Luchsinger, interview, May 4, 2022).

Chapter 4
Methodology

For topics with limited preceding research, an inductive research approach is recommended. Hereby, hypotheses can be deduced as a result of the research as opposed to testing hypotheses throughout the research. Consequently, due to the nature of the topic, an inductive exploratory research strategy was defined for the purpose of this paper. This strategy should allow for preliminary research on the topic of tokenization in real estate and create a basis for further, potentially deductive, research (Bortz & Döring, 2009). In line with the defined strategy, a qualitative approach was chosen. Qualitative research is often considered more open-ended than quantitative research. To ensure that the research is focused, it is recommended to define research questions in advance that can guide the work process. Ideally, the research questions should fill a gap in the current literature and follow a common logic (Bell et al., 2019, pp. 80, 83). As established at the beginning of the paper, the research questions are as follows:

RQ1: What is tokenization in real estate and how does it work? What are the underlying technologies? RQ2: What does the implementation of tokenization look like, opportunities and challenges?

RQ3: Case studies and expert interviews: What are the current best practices and lessons learnt?

RQ4: What recommendations can be given to different market participants going forward?

Throughout the research, both primary and secondary research were conducted. Below the research design and methods used for both are described in detail. The literature review and secondary research are discussed first as it presents the backbone of this paper and served as a basis for the following primary research. The primary research is then reviewed, it consists of three case studies and five expert interviews. Finally, the process of composing the conclusion and recommendations chapter is presented.

E. Schmid et al., *Tokenization in Real Estate*, SpringerBriefs in Finance,
https://doi.org/10.1007/978-3-031-55810-8_4

4.1 Literature Review and Secondary Research

The aim of the literature review and secondary research is primarily to establish a solid foundation on the understanding of tokenization in real estate and as a result answer RQ1 and RQ2. To do so, the paper starts with the technological background. This ensures that the basic underlying technologies, which enable tokenization in real estate (blockchain technology, distributed ledger technology, smart contracts, and tokenization) are considered and understood by the reader. The paper then continues with the concept of tokenization in real estate. Hereby, tokenization is first defined, and the different types of tokens are presented. The opportunities and potential applications are then analysed in detail and so are the current challenges and drawbacks. The most prominent challenge in most markets is the regulatory framework, it defines the limits of the potential application of tokenization in real estate. A separate chapter reviewing the legal foundation in Switzerland was added to specifically analyse the situation and potential in Switzerland. The real estate token market as a whole is then assessed, which includes an international outlook. Finally, some of the most recent developments in the general global market for digital assets are showcased, as developments within the digital asset sphere impact tokenization in real estate.

For both topics, technological background and tokenization in real estate, a subchapter, which specifically reviews academic work within these fields, was added. These two subchapters chronologically present what researchers have focused on so far and what conclusions they have drawn—as opposed to explaining the mechanics of the technologies or the specifics of tokenization, which is the subject matter of the following subchapters. This step ensures that the paper holds up to academic standards. The academic literature reviewed was retrieved using Google Scholar. The two topics of blockchain and tokenization in real estate as well as related/alternative keywords, for example, blockchain technology, distributed ledger technology (DLT), tokens, and tokenization of property were used to find relevant papers. Additionally, the sources of sources were reviewed. Relevant papers were in most cases published after the year 2008, so after the initial introduction of blockchain and Bitcoin by Satoshi Nakamoto. Indicators of quality were considered throughout the research process. Papers that have been peer-reviewed, cited by many others, and/or published in reputable journals were preferred.

The subchapters following the two literature reviews are based on digital sources outside of academic research as well. This is primarily the case for the topic of tokenization in real estate as the concept is new and not all advancements have yet been reviewed in an academic format. To still account for these, additional digital research was conducted using Google. Again, related or alternative terms to tokenization in real estate were used to find these sources, for example, tokenization, tokenization of assets, real estate tokenization, and real estate tokens. Generally, sources outside of the academic sphere are considered secondary, however, as established can be necessary due to the novelty of a subject matter. It further requires special attention to be paid to the credibility of the sources and quality of information (Bell et al., 2019, pp. 98–100). Consequently, a selective approach was used when collecting data throughout the secondary research, and predominately reports by reputable market participants such as Deloitte, EY, or RICS were used.

Overall, a literature review and secondary research are essential within academic research. While for quantitative research it is often a tool to deduce the hypotheses to be tested, it is also important for qualitative research as contextual knowledge. Hereby, it can help in understanding and contextualizing research results. When carrying out secondary research within a qualitative paper, the goal is to establish the current state of research in the specific field of study, what theories and concepts are discussed, and what are current debates and challenges (Flick, 2010, pp. 72–80). For this paper, the secondary research allowed a thorough understanding of tokenization in real estate, which was fundamental for the subsequent case studies and composing a constructive and goal-oriented interview guide.

4.2 Case Studies and Expert Interviews

In addition to secondary research, case studies were carried out as primary research. Specifically, a multiple-case study research design was chosen. Case studies are suitable for exploratory research and can allow for a more in-depth understanding of a situation as well as for studying a broader issue. Including multiple-case studies, furthermore, allows for comparisons to be made (Bell et al., 2019, pp. 64, 67). Specifically, three case studies of real estate assets located in Switzerland which have successfully been tokenized were carried out. The three case studies were chosen as they also represent the only Swiss properties to have been tokenized so far. The three case studies are:

- *Hello World*, located in Baar (ZG), tokenized by blockimmo
- *Bahnhofstrasse 52/B52*, located in Zurich (ZH), tokenized by BrickMark
- *Crowdlitoken Portfolio*, two properties located in Oensingen (SO) and Heimberg (BE), tokenized by Crodwlitoken

The case studies aim to answer RQ3. For this purpose, the case studies start with an overview of the tokenized assets. Then, the companies which carried out the tokenization processes are assessed. Here, documentation was chosen as a data collection research method. Then, as a further part of the case studies, expert interviews were conducted. Interviews as a research method are commonly found for the case study research design and can offer significant insights (Yin, 2014, pp. 105–113). Overall, the documentation provided necessary fundamental information on the cases, which could be reviewed and extended throughout the interviews.

The respective interview partners have all worked on the projects, allowing for a more in-depth understanding of the cases. In the case of Crowdlitoken two interviews were carried out as Dadvan Yousuf only had limited time, so Simon Büchi kindly offered to answer the remaining questions. Furthermore, Yousuf was CEO at the time of the interview but has since been relieved of all operational responsibilities. In addition, a fourth expert interview was carried out as part of the primary research. Dr. Catrina Luchsinger is a legal expert on the topics of digital assets and tokenization and could provide extensive information on the respective regulatory foundation in Switzerland. This was especially important as regulatory limitations and uncertainties represent some of the biggest challenges within the field. The interview partners are:

- *Bastiaan Don*, Founder and Managing Director of blockimmo (interviewed on 11. 04. 2022)
- *Stephan Rind*, Founder and CEO of BrickMark (interviewed on 10. 05. 2022)
- *Dadvan Yousuf*, CEO and Co-owner of Crowdlitoken (interviewed on 06. 04. 2022)
- *Simon Büchi*, CTO at Crowdlitoken (interviewed on 08. 04. 2022)
- *Dr. Catrina Luchsinger*, Partner at *MLL* (interviewed on 04. 05. 2022)

The expert interviews were conducted in a semi-standardized format. This means that the interviews followed approximately the same pre-defined structure. Before the interview, the aim of the paper, case studies, and expert interviews were explained. To start easy, the interview partners were prompted to recount how they were introduced to the topic of tokenization in real estate. The following questions, which made up the central part of the interviews, were then divided into three overarching themes: company-specific, case-specific, and personal opinions & recommendations. So, in addition to gaining further insights into the tokenization processes of the presented case studies, the interviews also aimed at collecting and understanding the experiences, perspectives, and opinions of active market participants. Finally, the interview partners were asked for a concluding comment on the topic. For the interview with Dr. Luchsinger the main themes were adjusted. Instead of company- and case-specific questions, questions about the legal foundation in Switzerland were asked. The introduction, conclusion, as well as the questions on personal opinions & recommendations remained the same. Subsequently, two slightly different interview guides were composed, both can be found in Appendix A.

Generally, a pre-defined structure can help guide interviews, ensuring that the relevant topic areas are discussed and a sound basis for comparison is created. However, the concept of a semi-structured interview simultaneously allows for flexibility where, for instance, follow-up questions can be added. It, furthermore, usually implies the use of open-ended questions (Bell et al., 2019, pp. 436, 438, 448). So, depending on the interview, the questions were not necessarily asked in exactly the same order or with precisely the same formulation. Instead, natural conversations where the experts could freely share their thoughts and views on the topic were held. In addition to semi-structured, the interviews can, furthermore, be considered cross-sectional. Indicating that they were conducted at one single point in time. The primary research design, therefore, does not follow a continued development of the cases but rather provides a current snapshot of the situation (Bell et al., 2019, p. 58).

The interviews were carried out at different times throughout the research process in accordance with the schedule of the respective interview partner. The interview with Bastiaan Don was held via Zoom. The interviews with Dr. Luchsinger and Stephan Rind were carried out in person. The interviews with Büchi and Yousuf took place in the form of phone calls. Overall, the interviews lasted around one hour, in the case of Büchi around 30 min, and for Yousuf around 15 min. Following the interviews, transcripts were written up in bullet point format. For this paper, a bullet point format was sufficient as the focus lay on 'what' the experts had to say on the topic as opposed to in what 'way' they said it. These transcripts can be found in Appendices B-F. The transcripts were then analysed, and the key messages were summarized in text, following the documented information on the case studies and respective companies.

4.3 Conclusion and Recommendations

In the conclusion and recommendations chapter, the defined research questions were answered drawing from all the gathered information. Additionally, RQ4 was approached. RQ4 attempts to give specific recommendations to market participants. Hereby, the results of RQ1-3 were analysed. This analysis revealed that it must first be established where the market should be heading in terms of tokenization in real estate. What implementations of blockchain and tokens within the real estate industry make sense and are beneficial to the market? While some of the analysed data indicate significant challenges and uncertainties, the potential of the concept, the conviction of the interviewed experts as well as recent market developments all point towards a wider adoption of tokenization in real estate in the future. Recommendations were, therefore, formed with the underlying assumption that many market participants will push for increased application and that these applications should aim towards realizing as many of the potential benefits of tokenization as possible. The resulting recommendations were defined with the Swiss market in mind, as the Swiss regulatory framework was specifically researched in more detail and regulations largely impact the current market situation and potential future developments. Furthermore, some of the recommendations apply to the market as a whole, while some were composed for specific market participants. Overall, the recommendations aim to capture the entirety of the real estate token market and include all relevant participants.

The results of qualitative research can be assessed using four criteria, as established by Lincoln and Guba: credibility, transferability, dependability, and confirmability. In terms of credibility, this paper achieves data triangulation by using both secondary and primary research. Furthermore, the primary research entails multiple-case studies as well as multiple expert interviews. The transferability of the results to the Swiss market as a whole is strong, as the case studies include all use cases in the market. However, it is limited on a global level. To ensure dependability, thorough research on the topic of tokenization in real estate was carried out, as the topic is still narrow most aspects could be covered. Additionally, in line with the inductive research strategy, a flexible and open manner was kept throughout the research process. Finally, for confirmability, an objective attitude throughout the research process as well as towards the results generated was fundamental and kept as well as possible (Bell et al., 2019, pp. 363–365).

Chapter 5
Case Studies and Expert Interviews

In this chapter, three case studies on tokenized real estate properties in Switzerland are presented. Each case study starts with an introduction to the tokenized property as well as the basics of the tokenization process. The companies which managed the tokenization are then assessed, including the legal and technical basis on which they carried out the process. In a second step, interviews that were carried out with the respective founders or representatives of management to gain additional insight into the tokenization of real estate in Switzerland are summarized. The summaries further focus on reflecting the interviewees' opinions on best practices, lessons learnt, and crucial aspects going forward.

5.1 Case Study I: Hello World

Hello World is a single real estate asset at Grabenstrasse 3 in Baar, Switzerland. The property consists of 18 apartments and a restaurant. Around 20% of the asset or CHF 3 million was tokenized and sold in 2019 by blockimmo to four different investors in a club deal. The deal was carried out in partnership with Swiss Crypto Tokens and Elea Labs (Don, 2021). Swiss Crypto Tokens made the deal possible with their CryptoFranc (XCHF), which is pegged to the Swiss franc and therefore offers stability—a stablecoin. Elea Labs, a proptech company, contributed validated data about the property. Finally, the deal was carried out on the Ethereum blockchain and verified on blockimmo's platform (moneycab, 2019).

E. Schmid et al., *Tokenization in Real Estate*, SpringerBriefs in Finance,
https://doi.org/10.1007/978-3-031-55810-8_5

5.1.1 blockimmo

The tokenization and sale of Hello World were coordinated by blockimmo. blockimmo was founded by Bastiaan Don in 2018. Don has since expanded the business and blockimmo is now part of Token Factory Ltd. based in Zug (Don, interview, April 11, 2022). While their focus currently lies on Token Factory, the initial business model for blockimmo is still presented below for the purpose of this case study.

Blockimmo's vision is to be 'A global real estate market far more efficient than the stock market today' and their mission is to 'Be the global marketplace for real estate tokenization'. (blockimmo, n.d.). In short, they aim to increase the efficiency of transactions between sellers and investors of real estate. According to blockimmo, such transactions are currently slowed down by the need for intermediaries, such as banks and notaries, creating a bottleneck and resulting in higher costs for both parties. blockimmo sees enormous potential in using blockchain and smart contracts for real estate transactions and investments to increase efficiency while continuing to ensure a safe business environment. In their white paper (blockimmo, 2018), they describe further advantages, many of which were already discussed in Sect. 3.3. For example, easier access to real estate investments, especially at considerably smaller stakes, and better liquidity.

In terms of implementation, the owner of a property can contact blockimmo to have their asset (partly) sold via the blockimmo platform, using blockchain technology. Once listed on the platform, a smart contract managing the property creates a token and mints a maximum of one million of them. These tokens represent the ownership and rights to the property and are then sold via a crowd-sale. If a minimum amount is sold in a pre-determined timespan, the crowd-sale was successful. The tokens can, however, not be transferred until the property has been verified on blockimmo's on-chain land register, and blockimmo has carried out all necessary legal processes off-chain. Blockimmo's own on-chain land register registers each owner with a smart contract and identifies them with their on-chain profile, which each investor has to create before investing on blockimmo's platform. The federal government can connect to the on-chain register with their own profile and holds certain rights. Off-chain, the property has to, for the time being, go through the same administrative process which is required for any change in property ownership in Switzerland, as explained in Sect. 3.5. Here, blockimmo promises to fully act in the interest of the investors. Currently, the number of owners possible per property in the Swiss land register is limited and changing the way the land register is managed will take time and effort (the final goal is to have the Swiss land register transition on-chain in its entirety). For the time being, the tokenized properties will, therefore, be held by a Liechtenstein-based fund. For each property, a separate fund and a separate token are issued (blockimmo, 2018). This legal format was approved by the Swiss government on December 7, 2018, in the legal framework for blockchain and distributed ledger technology (DLT) (The Federal Council, 2018). Additionally, blockimmo has also added anti-money laundering (AML) and know your customer (KYC) features.

Once all legal matters are taken care of, the investors receive their tokens. They pay for their tokens using the cryptocurrency Ether (ETH) and their tokens are stored in their hardware wallets. The tokens are designed to support a decentralized autonomous organization (DAO) with multiple owners. A property management company is initially appointed by blockimmo but can be changed if a majority of token holders agree. The income generated with the property is directly distributed to the owners via smart contracts and paid out in ETH. Should an investor wish to sell all or parts of their ownership, blockimmo is working on the peer-to-peer trading platform STX.SWISS, which will operate on the Ethereum blockchain (blockimmo, 2018).

Overall, blockimmo aims to create their services and platforms as user-friendly as possible. blockimmo, therefore, works on three layers. Layer 1 being the blockchain and smart contracts, layer 2 is a blockchain interface, enabling interaction with the blockchain, and finally layer 3, the blockimmo frontend, so their website or dApp (blockimmo, 2018). Updates and improvements to their platforms are continuously introduced. Enabling, for example, payment with the stablecoin DAI as well as with fiat currency through PayPal (Dietz, 2019). So far, blockimmo has tokenized and cooperated the sale of one property, 'Hello World' in Baar, Switzerland. blockimmo aims to start with tokenizing further Swiss properties and then move their target focus abroad (blockimmo, 2018).

5.1.2 *Interview: Bastiaan Don*

Bastiaan Don was interviewed on April 11, 2022, via a Zoom call. The interview transcript can be found in Appendix C. Don founded a company with a friend throughout their studies, renting out furnished apartments to expats on the internet. They developed the software themselves and made sure everything could be processed online. As a result, they gained a lot of experience in the real estate field. A fascination for blockchain and Bitcoin followed. Don then decided to combine the two and founded blockimmo (2018).

The goal, initially, was to demonstrate that blockchain can be implemented in a regulated market and be compliant with said regulations without giving up on decentralization. The project should further better the accessibility of the asset class and enable everyone to invest in real estate. Moreover, it could provide real estate owners with another capital market for liquidity. Finally, blockimmo wanted to create a secondary market for the fractionalized shares of real estate with their project STX.SWISS.

Right off the bat, blockimmo was able to start with its first property, Hello World in Zug. For this property, blockimmo chose to tokenize 20% of the asset, both to bypass some of the regulatory difficulties with the land register and to show how an owner could liquidate only part of a real estate asset. blockimmo, furthermore, chose to tokenize equity instead of debt as debt represents a higher risk for investors. Finally, they chose a fund structure based in Liechtenstein, where at the time more specific guidelines were in place. Here, they worked with Bank Frick and the Financial Market Authority (FMA). They also communicated with the Swiss Financial Market Supervisory Authority (FINMA) to showcase how such a project was carried out.

In the end, the transaction was not what blockimmo had initially set out to achieve. Four investors decided to take part in the transaction. As it did not make sense to set up a fund structure for only four investors and one single property basic contract between the investors and seller were drawn up. The transaction itself was, however, carried out smoothly and without any financial intermediary. Throughout the entire process, the biggest challenge was to adhere to regulations that had not yet been finalized. Also, not being able to directly tokenize the asset was limiting. Nevertheless, blockimmo wanted to prove that the technology itself works and show what a transaction carried out via a blockchain could look like.

In retrospect, Don stated that it was probably too early for the tokenization of real estate assets. However, they are still convinced of the potential of blockchain technology. The business has now been re-named and re-positioned as Token Factory. They have moved away from Swiss real estate and instead capitalize on their established tokenization solution for securities. Hereby, Token Factory acts as a technology provider and does consultancy on a variety of projects. They, for example, tokenized the first fund in Liechtenstein with Bank Frick and are currently working on a gold-backed project as well as in the wine industry. Furthermore, they are still working on STX.SWISS and are in close contact with FINMA to enable decentralized trading for regulated assets. In terms of real estate, they are currently looking at high-yield properties in Eastern Europe, offering owners a solution to liquidate parts of their portfolio using a fund structure. They see potential in this strategy as it offers high yields and a safe structure to investors, at the same time, the owners do not need to sell their properties to withdraw capital from their assets. When launching the product, they want to ensure that a secondary market with substantial liquidity is available from day one. So, an investor can invest in real estate with their cryptocurrency, receive monthly payouts, and liquidate their investment at any time.

On a more general note, the industry is faced with some key challenges. First of all, many don't understand the concept of tokenizing securities. Then, there are the missing secondary markets. Even if an investor is convinced of the potential of blockchain and tokens and is ready to invest, they will still want to know that they can exit that investment. Don believes that there first needs to be a secondary market exchange for regulated digital securities and then discussions around which securities should be tokenized can be held. Hereby, real estate will probably be one of the last assets to be tokenized. Also, the usability of the current infrastructure needs improvement, an Ethereum wallet, for example, is not necessarily user-friendly. Finally, in Switzerland, the land register poses a problem. It currently only recognizes a natural or juridical person as a potential owner, there would need to be a third option that would allow, for example, a smart contract to hold the asset. As a result, the direct tokenization of a real estate asset is not an option right now. Consequently, tokenizing the shares of a company holding the asset is the easiest way to go. To move development further, Don believes that someone needs to be willing to take the risk and tokenize a big portfolio (provided there is a secondary market).

Overall, investor interest is currently high and there are a lot of announcements, partnerships, and so on, happening on the market. Unfortunately, however, there is often not a lot of substance to these news. Many of the big players are not actually interested in the technology but they need to showcase their innovative side, resulting limited actual actions. A distinction must be made between a real blockchain and everything else which is just trying to ride the wave. According to Don, the fact that a blockchain can't be controlled by a centralized entity is the core fundament of blockchain. So, if at the end of the day a hand full of banks or countries are controlling the main blockchain infrastructure, we haven't achieved what we wanted to.

Finally, in terms of a global outlook, the USA is making progress with, for example, MakerDAO. Also, the EU's MiCA draft is promising but not yet in force. On the other side, however, there are jurisdictions that have put strong regulations or bans on blockchain and cryptocurrencies.

5.2 Case Study II: Bahnhofstrasse 52/B52

The case of Bahnhofstrasse 52, also known as B52, encompasses a single property in the city of Zürich of around 1600 sqm at, as the name suggests, Bahnhofstrasse 52. RFR Holdings sold the asset to BrickMark in a share deal in January 2020. BrickMark purchased 80% of the shares of Bahnhofstrasse AG (which holds the property), they additionally held a call option to acquire the remaining shares within 9 months. The property is a commercial real estate asset with high redevelopment potential. The redevelopment is led by RFR Holdings, which will continue to hold 20% of the shares. The redevelopment is expected to be completed in early 2023. Of the initial purchase, 20% was paid for with BrickMark's own BrickMark Tokens (BMT), a hybrid security token. At around EUR 130 million total purchasing price, this represents the largest completed real estate transaction on a blockchain. BrickMark's CEO Stephan Rind has stated that RFR Holdings' interest in innovating the real estate market with tokenization was, without doubt, helpful for the success of the transaction (BrickMark AG, 2020). Furthermore, the general interest in the transaction proved to be enormous. Rind spoke of 400–1000 inquiries by investors from all over the world per day, for a period of multiple weeks after issuing a press release on the transaction (Stefano, 2021).

5.2.1 BrickMark

BrickMark is a commercial real estate investment firm based in Zug. The company was founded by CEO Stephan Rind in 2018 (Stefano, 2021). BrickMark says 'We provide universal access to the world's premier real estate in a digital way. Secure and efficient'. In addition to the property on Bahnhofstrasse they state to currently have EUR 1bn of real estate investments for tokenization in their pipeline (BrickMark, n.d.). BrickMark already stated their continued interest to acquire high-quality commercial real estate properties in major European and North American cities when issuing a press release on the transaction of Bahnhofstrasse 52 in 2020 (BrickMark AG, 2020).

Throughout this process, the BMT is intended to work as the preferred source of financing. The BMTs are based on the Ethereum blockchain with an ERC-20 token standard. The tokens are underpinned by a security, a subordinated perpetual bond, which is backed by the BrickMark real estate portfolio, and held by a special purpose vehicle (SPV). Smart contracts are coded on top of the securities on the blockchain and used to establish ownership rights. They also allow for the owners to claim their share of the income the property generates on a quarterly basis (BrickMark AG, 2020). According to the Tokenist (Fries, 2021), the price of a BMT will be based on the portfolio's net asset value performance. Token holders can, therefore, profit from the appreciation of the underlying assets. Legal and regulatory compliance is ensured by BrickMark when acquiring the asset and incorporating it into an SPV. BrickMark, furthermore, aims for high transparency and has been accepted by the European Public Real Estate Association (EPRA). The frequent reporting by BrickMark follows the EPRA best practice guidelines (BrickMark AG, 2020).

Currently, the BMT has not yet been listed and is not available to investors. Should additional BMTs be issued and offered in a security token offering (STO), the accrued funds will be used for the acquisition of additional properties and be held in a deposit account in the meantime. Investments will then be possible in either a fiat currency, ETH, or Bitcoin. As a result, each issued BMT has an underlying value, either in the form of cash or in real estate assets and no additional BMTs can be issued without such an underlying value. Once the BMT is listed, token holders can trade them and potentially make capital gains if there is an increase in the price. However, price fluctuations should be significantly smaller in comparison with cryptocurrency as the tokens represent a real value (Rind, 2021a, pp. 100–101).

More recently, according to the Neue Zürcher Zeitung, BrickMark is working with the token and decentralized finance expert DSENT, a venture of Inacta, an IT firm based in Zug (Stefano, 2021). DSENT is expected to launch the platform Tokengate in the summer of 2022. Tokengate is anticipated to be a one-stop shop to create, sell, buy, and manage tokens of a range of assets (Tokengate, n.d.). The two companies are setting up the platform BrickGate in a joint venture. BrickGate offers tokenization services to other companies in cooperation with the Swiss bank InCore (Rind, 2021b). Rind, furthermore, spoke at the *Real Estate Investment und Asset Management* symposium on May 03, 2022, in Rotkreuz, Switzerland, and explained how BrickMark will continue to acquire real estate assets. Amongst others, BrickMark recently acquired Castle Collection S.A. Naturally, these assets (castles) are quite special properties and as a result lend themselves well to creating interesting investment opportunities. With the help of smart contracts, an investment opportunity could be combined with other benefits in the form of, for example, a membership which would allow special access to events or better hotel rates (Rind, 2022).

5.2.2 Interview: Stephan Rind

Stephan Rind was interviewed in person in Zollikon, Switzerland on May 10, 2022. The interview transcript can be found in Appendix D. Rind started to read up on blockchain and crypto around 2017 and was quickly convinced by the potential of the technology. The decentralization aspect and trustless environment were especially fascinating. The idea of putting an illiquid asset such as real estate on a blockchain, making it directly accessible to retail investors, and largely decreasing transaction costs, started to form and Rind decided to establish BrickMark.

The goal behind BrickMark was to create a digital real estate company. So far, the company has tokenized one asset, B52. Convincing the seller to accept BMT as payment was the biggest challenge, RFR Holding has no guarantee that the token will ever be listed or will ever be worth anything to other investors. However, carrying out such a transaction with a large global player was an important step as it sent a strong message to the market. Another challenge was the regulatory aspect. The DLT Act was not yet in place and BrickMark had to put a lot of money and effort into developing a suitable business model and prospectus together with various legal experts. Often the legal experts weren't sure either what requirements would need to be met and FINMA could take months to respond as they were trying to create the respective framework. Since then, the token industry in Switzerland has evolved. Now there are product structures available for which clear regulations are in place.

Moreover, the general climate around tokenization and digital assets has changed for the better in jurisdictions such as Switzerland, Germany, or Luxembourg. Also, corporations such as J. P. Morgan or Goldman Sachs have started to research and implement the blockchain technology, showing that resulting innovations can benefit all players in the market by saving costs, increasing efficiency, and potentially even creating more intelligent products, and offering new alternative investment opportunities.

One of the main tasks right now is education. Once someone has understood how the technology works, they usually start to see all the potential benefits and applications and are quickly convinced. From an owner's perspective, BrickMark has received more inquiries over the past 9-12 months than they can properly work through. From an investor's perspective, however, it is more difficult. Many will argue that they might just as well invest in a traditional real estate fund. Creating an incentive for private investors to invest in real estate-backed tokens and explaining how tokens can offer access to new assets and allow for more customization is crucial.

Nevertheless, according to Rind, market experts agree that there will be significant development and expansion of the token industry. The offers for digital securities will increase, illiquid assets will be tokenized and a functioning secondary market available. The question is how fast it will happen and not if it will happen. The timeline will largely depend on how quickly the different countries can outline a regulatory framework. To the overall market Rind recommends that companies should have a designated employee focused on digitalization and blockchain. That person can educate the rest of the team and then clients can be introduced to the topic as well. In terms of a global outlook, non-fungible token (NFT) sales of real estate are already happening in the USA. Meanwhile, Germany is also developing strongly. In Dubai, a new DLT act should be coming into force this year and Australia is setting up an exchange similar to the SIX Digital Exchange (SDX).

In addition to BrickMark, Rind has also founded BrickGate. BrickGate aims to become the biggest marketplace for real estate-backed tokens in Europe, sort of an Amazon for real estate. BrickGate will work with, for example, developers to help them raise capital for their projects. Hereby, BrickGate will manage the set-up of the platform, guide clients in making the right choices for their business model (e.g., should debt or equity be tokenized), and issue the respective tokens. The platform is connected with InCore bank which can handle payments made in fiat currencies. Clients could, furthermore, choose to have BrickGate take care of the lifecycle management of the tokens as well. So, have them manage the tokens following the issuance. For BrickMark, this will generate a recurrent stream of revenue. Apart from working with developers, real estate agents could have their clients' properties tokenized and put on the BrickGate platform (not necessarily in a fractionalized form) as well. Other agents connected to the platform could access these properties and present them to their clients. This concept increases the reach of the first agent and the range of offers of the second. It greatly expands the often very local market of real estate.

In short, BrickGate aims to create a cross-border marketplace. Within this business model BrickGate receives a fee for structuring the process, placement, minting, and often also a success fee and token management fee. They are open to receiving up to 50% of these fees in the form of the tokens which are issued for the project. Only registered (KYC) investors can invest in the tokens and should they decide to transfer some of their tokens, the new owner will also need to register and BrickGate will need to be notified about the exchange as interest or dividends are only paid out to registered investors. Currently, there are projects valued at around $2 billion in the pipeline.

5.3 Case Study III: Crowdlitoken Portfolio

Crowdlitoken acquires real estate assets to then tokenize and offer them on their platform in a fractionalized manner. With a minimum investment of CHF 100, anyone can invest and buy their tokens (CRT). It is up to the investor to choose which property they would like to invest in. Crowdlitoken has so far bought and tokenized two real estate assets. The first property was added to the Crowdlitoken portfolio in

2020. It is located in Oensingen, Solothurn and is currently estimated to be worth CHF 9.3 million. The second property is located in Heimberg, Bern and is valued at around CHF 5.6 million. Both are commercial properties and were financed through Crowdlitoken's first financing round and issuance of 16 million CRTs, raised through a DPO (digital product offering) (Crowdlitoken (c)).

5.3.1 Crowdlitoken

Crowdlitoken is a Liechtenstein-based digital real estate token investment platform, it is the 'First European provider of a digital financial investment for real estate'. Crowdli AG was founded in 2016, followed by Crowdlitoken AG in 2018 (Crowdlitoken (a)). The first financing round was carried out in 2020 and CHF 16 million worth of tokens were issued and sold to around 450 investors (Crowdlitoken, 2020). In the same year, the first property in Oensingen, Solothurn was acquired, and the world's first investor portal was launched. Dadvan Yousuf was then named the new CEO in fall 2021 (Crowdlitoken (a)). However, Yousuf stirred interest in the media around inconsistencies in the narrative of how they became a crypto millionaire as a teenager (Pauli & Jaquemart, 2022). Most recently, FINMA halted the listing of Yousuf's cryptocurrency Dohrnii (DHN) (Hopf-Sulc, 2022) and Bern's public prosecutor's office opened proceedings on suspicion of fraud and money laundering (Pauli, 2022). As a result, Yousuf has been relieved of all operational responsibilities at Crowdlitoken AG and is no longer part of the board of directors at Crowdli AG (Hässig, 2022).

If an investor is interested in buying CRTs and investing in one or multiple properties on the Crowdlitoken platform, they first need to go through a registration process. They can then buy CRTs and place the desired amount (minimum of CHF 100 worth of CRTs, currently at 1 CRT = CHF 1) in the desired property. Following their investment, the investor receives their share of the income generated on a monthly basis (CRT-Cash) or can choose to reinvest that return for a higher share in the property (CRT-Reinvest). More specifically, the underlying subordinate bonds are issued at a minimum return of 0.825% in years 1 and 2, 1.4875% in year 3, and 2.1% from year 4 and onwards. Should an investor wish to divest they can trade their shares over the Crowdlitoken platform if there is matching demand. Alternatively, they can get repaid at the end of the investment period on December 14, 2044 (25-year term) for their respective share. The exact amount will depend on the value of the properties at that point but will be at least CHF 0.7 per token (Crowdlitoken (b)).

Crowdlitoken aims to frequently add new properties to their selection of investment opportunities. The detailed real estate strategy document (Crowdlitoken, 2019) outlines their approach to doing so. A country strategy, for example, is described in more detail: investments will initially focus on commercial properties in Switzerland (bearing in mind Lex Koller) and commercial and residential properties in Germany. The strategy then adds Austria in a second phase, and in a third phase countries outside of the DACH region. Further elements of the overarching strategy include the acquisition process, due diligence, purchasing and sale decisions, and asset management. Crowdlitoken, furthermore, guarantees legal and regulatory compliance when adding a new property to their portfolio. Following the coming into force of the Token and VT Service Providers Act in 2020, Crowdlitoken was approved by the FMA in Liechtenstein at the end of 2020 and is now officially registered as a blockchain company in the country (Crowdlitoken, 2021). Finally, Crowdlitoken partnered with Upvest at the end of 2020 to offer their investors an easy custody solution in the form of a wallet to directly store their investments. Their application programming interface (API) also provides further digital infrastructure and takes care of cybersecurity aspects (Upvest, 2020). Other partnerships include SygnEx, who support the creation of a legally compliant trading platform for Crowdlitoken's bonds (Crowdlitoken, 2020b).

5.3.2 Interview: Dadvan Yousuf

Dadvan Yousuf is the CEO and co-owner of Crowdlitoken. The interview with Yousuf took place on April 6, 2022, in the form of a phone call. Unfortunately, due to time constraints, the interview only lasted around 15 minutes. For that reason, not all sections of the interview guide could be covered. A focus was put on discussing Yousuf's personal opinions and recommendations in the context of real estate tokenization, both in Switzerland and in a global setting. The respective interview transcript can be found in Appendix E.

Yousuf stated that the purpose of Crowdlitoken is to democratize the real estate asset class. Everyone should be able to part take in the real estate investment market, even with just a CHF 100. While they still want to continue to work with Crowdlitoken's current business model, the company wants to add other services in the future. Yousuf was vague around the exact concept, however, it could go in the direction of offering a platform where individuals can tokenize their homes and/or find alternative financing for their homes.

In terms of the general development of the real estate token industry, Yousuf does not see regulatory concerns as a key element to either facilitate or hinder the development of the industry. According to many market participants, the largest challenge is that people don't know what a token is, and have a lack of understanding for most possibilities in crypto and blockchain. This lack of understanding leads to a lack of trust and interest in taking advantage of investment opportunities within the sphere. However, asset-backed tokens such as real estate tokens should be easier to explain than cryptocurrencies, hence Yousuf's interest in this specific market. Yousuf is, furthermore, the CEO of Dohrnii, a platform focused on educating retail investors about the crypto industry.

Yousuf further assesses the Swiss real estate market to be highly attractive to international investors. However, many investments are limited by Lex Koller/ Friedrich regulations. This could be bypassed through tokenization and fractionalization, allowing a foreign investor to own part of a Swiss residential property. In general, Yousuf believes that the Lex Koller/Friedrich regulations are discriminating against international investors and should be changed. On a global level, tokens will be used for the healthy diversification of most portfolios, meaning portfolios will include assets such as NFTs, and/or various security tokens such as real estate-backed tokens. These tokens, however, will most likely not be a direct tokenization of the asset but represent tokenized economic rights related to the ownership of the asset. So, for example, tokenized debt. Having said that, the industry is still in its very beginnings. Yousuf is convinced that tokenization in real estate is the future, they see a broader application within the next 5 years, approximately.

5.3.3 *Interview: Simon Büchi*

As a result of the limited interview with Dadvan Yousuf a second interview within the Crowdlitoken Portfolio case study was carried out. Simon Büchi, CTO at Crowdlitoken, offered to discuss the more company- and case-specific questions in the interview guide. The interview took place on April 8, 2022, also in the form of a phone call. The transcript of the interview can be found in Appendix F.

Crowdlitoken's main goal is to offer investment possibilities even with just a small budget. Crowdlitoken would not necessarily need to work on a blockchain, but it is a well-fitting solution. Overall, the aim is to tokenize and offer as many properties on the platform as possible and offer as many investment opportunities as possible. Here, the main elements to ensure success still include many traditional business tasks such as carrying out a proficient valuation and finding suitable investment opportunities. The current Crowdlitoken portfolio consists of two commercial properties, neither are special nor exciting but they are good investments, and they generate good returns. Then, instead of selling the property through an intermediary, it is sold directly to the investors. For this part to work, the technology, the platform, and the tokenization process need to be reliable and work seamlessly. While this is not rocket science anymore, it still required some trial and error. Overall, Crowdlitoken does not want to be a new fancy investment opportunity for tech nerds interested in crypto but a modern and secure investment platform comparable to a pillar 3a investment app.

The biggest challenges when tokenizing the two properties were compliance and legal aspects. Putting together the prospectus, getting the right licences, and making sure the business model would be approved by FINMA took a lot of time and effort. Meanwhile, a current challenge is the continuous onboarding of new investors. While there has been a lot of interest in Crowdlitoken, new investors first need to be made aware of the investment opportunities, understand the concept, and be convinced of it. So, while there is a pipeline for further properties to be tokenized, the focus right now is to increase investments in the first two properties.

With the change in CEO, there is a new financing strategy in the works. Currently, Crowdlitoken is buying real estate with its own equity and by getting a mortgage—so traditional real estate financing. However, with this strategy, you need a lot of equity. The new strategy aims to reserve the property from the seller for around 1–2 months. Within this timeframe, investors could buy tokens and place them on the respective property. If enough tokens are invested, the property can then be bought by Crowdlitoken and be put on their platform. A type of crowdfunding strategy. Still, naturally, around 50% of financing would come from a mortgage. At first, both strategies are most likely going to be applied side-by-side. Should the crowdfunding strategy work well, they might switch entirely.

Overall, Büchi stated that there is increasing demand for less capital-intensive investment opportunities as well as for real estate as an asset class. The concept of tokenization is still very new and Crowdlitoken might not have found the best way to tokenize an asset; however, all companies currently work on a trial-and-error basis. Still, Büchi is convinced of the future of tokenization as tokenizing a non-liquid asset like real estate can truly create benefits.

Chapter 6
Conclusion and Recommendations

In the following chapter, the research questions defined at the very beginning of this paper are reviewed and answered, by drawing from all the information gathered throughout both the secondary and primary research. As part of RQ4, the consequent recommendations to market participants are formed.

6.1 RQ1: What Is Tokenization in Real Estate and How Does It Work? What Are the Underlying Technologies?

Tokenization in real estate refers to a digital representation of a real estate asset in the form of a token, enabled through blockchain technology. The holder of the token is also the owner of the asset. The token can, therefore, also be understood as the digital representation of ownership. If the asset is tokenized as a whole, a so-called non-fungible token or NFT is created. However, blockchain technology, often in combination with smart contracts, also allows for the fractionalization of an asset. Meaning, that instead of just creating one token the issuer can choose how many parts the asset should be divided into and create the respective number of tokens. Such tokens can then be considered fungible tokens and are the digital representation of one share of that real estate asset.

The above-described concept, however, is often difficult to apply in practice due to regulatory limitations which do not allow for the direct tokenization of a real estate asset; there are distinct laws in place determining how the ownership, as well as the transfer of ownership, of a real estate asset is to be handled. The direct tokenization and fractionalization of a real estate asset, especially also when assuming a large number of different owners and continuous transactions, does not comply with these laws. As a result, an additional layer between the asset and the owner(s) is composed, an intermediate structure that holds the asset. It is then not the asset that is tokenized but either the equity, debt, or an economic interest of that intermediate

E. Schmid et al., *Tokenization in Real Estate*, SpringerBriefs in Finance,
https://doi.org/10.1007/978-3-031-55810-8_6

entity. So, while many imply the direct tokenization (and often also fractionalization) of an asset when referring to tokenization in real estate, a distinction needs to be made when reviewing current use cases and possibilities in the market as an additional layer of ownership will usually have been established.

In terms of underlying technologies, distributed ledger technology (DLT), blockchain, and smart contracts are the core technological elements enabling the tokenization of a security such as real estate. Their main characteristics are briefly summarized next.

DLT: Various DLT solutions have been created but blockchain is by far the most known. In short, DLT is a shared record of data and presents an alternative solution to processing and storing data. The main characteristic distinguishing a DLT solution is first and foremost the decentralization of the system, which entails that the system does not require a central entity to check the activities of its participants. Instead, it works as a peer-to-peer network in a trustless environment. Hereby, the participants reach a consensus on the correctness of the shared data by using a consensus mechanism/algorithm to verify the validity of each new set of information. Each participant then holds a copy of the created ledger. As a result, the shared data is considered transparent and immutable, making it a very secure system for storing and processing data. It, furthermore, allows for the participants of the network to carry out peer- to-peer transactions without the need for a trusted intermediary as asymmetric cryptographic proof substitutes for such an intermediary. While DLT solutions have mostly been implemented within financial markets, the presented benefits should allow for a range of applications. Suggestions for alternative areas of application have been made including the healthcare industry, manufacturing, and the government.

Blockchain: Blockchain is a type of DLT and therefore holds the same characteristics as described above. Blockchain was introduced by Nakamoto (2008) together with the cryptocurrency Bitcoin to enable non-reversible financial transactions on a peer-to-peer basis which do not rely upon financial institutions as a trusted third party and where the double-spending issue is bypassed with the proof-of- work (PoW) consensus mechanism. For blockchain specifically, the added and verified (transaction) data is stored in blocks in chronological order where each block refers to the preceding block. Multiple ways to classify blockchains have been suggested. The simplest is a division into permissioned and permissionless blockchains. A permissionless blockchain is a public blockchain, indicating that anyone can join and be active in the network. A permissioned blockchain indicates a private network. While the characteristics of blockchain are promising and a range of beneficial applications should be possible, there are also challenges to be considered. These include, for example, scalability, security, and sustainability concerns. Details on blockchain architecture, the process of adding a new block, and current challenges have been presented in Sect. 2.3.

Smart Contracts: DLT solutions such as blockchain offer an ideal basis for the application of smart contracts. Smart contracts are programmes that automatically execute contract clauses when pre-defined conditions are met in a predictable manner. From a technical perspective, a smart contract can be programmed to carry out whatever actions have been agreed upon. Consequently, the potential areas of application are vast, and suggestions have been made for the public sector, distributed system security, and the financial industry. Smart contracts also allow for hybrid tokens to give their holders special benefits or access. Within the field of real estate, smart contracts can be used to automate tasks in, for example, property management or decentralized autonomous organization (DAS). Overall, smart contracts can allow to bypass intermediaries and increase efficiency for a range of tasks and as a result, significantly decrease costs. Smart contracts are, furthermore, considered transparent to the network, immutable, and less prone to human error. However, as with blockchain technology, there are challenges to consider. These include the readability of smart contract code, potential bugs within the code and their consequences as well as the trustworthiness of oracles.

6.2 RQ2: What Does the Implementation of Tokenization Look Like, Opportunities and Challenges?

The implementation of tokenization in real estate has been analysed considering the level of integration of blockchain(s) on a scale of 0–8, where level 0 refers to no integration of blockchain and level 8 illustrates a scenario in which the blockchains of various countries and jurisdictions work together, enabling peer-to-peer transactions of fractionalized real estate across different blockchains and borders (see Sect. 3.3, pp. 29–30). While there is no use case for a level 8 integration it does, in theory, allow for a wide range of applications. For owners, tokenizing and fractionalizing their asset(s) could give them the opportunity to withdraw parts of their capital while continuing to hold the asset. Instead of freeing capital, tokenization could also represent an alternative to traditional ways of raising capital, both for institutional real estate investors and for private individuals looking to purchase a home. This alternative way of raising capital could, furthermore, be applied to development projects as well.

When implementing blockchain and tokenization in the real estate market in one of the described ways, a series of benefits can potentially be seized. The fractionalization lowers the entry barrier for retail investors, democratizing an asset class that is traditionally hard to access. This in turn increases liquidity as it adds a large pool of new potential investors that can invest directly and without an intermediary. As a result, owners might benefit from a liquidity premium and investors from an additional source of capital. The possibility of investing directly and with low capital requirements further offers higher customization of investments and potentially increased diversification. Meanwhile, blockchain technology increases data transparency and in turn security, and in combination with smart contracts, tasks can be automated, for example, throughout the due diligence process. The automation of tasks as well as the increased transparency, access to capital, increased liquidity, and the potential elimination of certain intermediaries such as brokers or lawyers all allow for an increase in efficiency as well as cost reductions throughout real estate investment and real estate transaction processes.

In practice, the implementation of tokenization can be divided into multiple steps. First, the deal needs to be structured according to the needs and aims of the issuer. Considerations should include which jurisdictions and therefore which regulations will be relevant, the intermediate structure, what is being tokenized (equity, debt, or an economic interest), the fee structure, number of tokens, and price per token, as well as the rights and obligations of token holders. Next, the digitization phase consists of setting up the blockchain, and coding and adding the necessary smart contracts. Again, a series of decisions must be made including choosing a blockchain protocol, token standard, and custody solution. The primary distribution of the tokens or security token offering (STO) can then be initiated. In this step, anti-money laundering (AML) and know your customer (KYC) regulations might apply. Investors will usually purchase tokens with cryptocurrencies and then store them in their wallets. On the blockchain, a digital register of members (ROM) is created, serving as a record of ownership. The following post-tokenization management includes automated processes such as dividend distribution and shareholder voting enabled by smart contracts. Issuers will often have a tool or dashboard to keep track of their blockchain and tokens. Finally, a token holder can decide to liquidate their investment by selling their tokens to another investor on a peer-to-peer basis, assuming there is a suitable secondary market exchange.

In Switzerland, this process needs to be carried out in compliance with a series of regulatory guidelines. This includes the administrative structure (land register and cadastre) and laws around the ownership and transfer of real estate (requiring an adjustment in the land register, a public deed, and a notary). It also includes the newly introduced DLT Act, which came into force in 2021 in a two-step process. Most importantly, the act introduced a new form of uncertificated security and allowed for the issuing of licences for DLT trading facilities. In international comparison, Switzerland has a well-developed framework for DLT solutions and digital securities, including the taxation of such securities. However, as the act is new there have not been many use cases showcasing how the regulations apply in practice and there are still regulatory gaps to be filled. Here, a non-action letter to the Financial Market Supervisory Authority (FINMA) could come into play to resolve such uncertainties. Regulations might also differ depending on the chosen legal structure of the intermediate ownership entity, the location and therefore jurisdiction of the underlying real estate asset, and the type of investors. For intermediate structures, a real estate fund, a limited partnership for collective investment, a real estate company for qualified or unqualified investors, or an SPV are the basic models to choose from. They each have different legal requirements, advantages, and disadvantages.

Considering the different opportunities for application, the potential benefits, and the comparably well- regulated environment in Switzerland, tokenization in real estate should be flourishing. However, there are also challenges to overcome, making market participants hesitant around tokenization, and hindering a wider application. Especially on a global level, there are still many regulatory issues to consider. Land registers don't allow for the direct tokenization of assets but intermediate structures tear at the benefits of tokenization. There might also be political opposition to, for example, the digitization of the land register as directly tokenized and fractionalized real estate assets could lead to even higher property prices. Furthermore, some market participants benefit from the current illiquidity and information asymmetry of real estate. Then the technical challenges of blockchain and smart contracts need to be considered as well, as the technology needs to work seamlessly for a wider adoption to be successful. Also, participants need to trust the underlying technological elements such as the blockchain protocol, as most investors don't have the necessary knowledge to check the code themselves. Next, issuing tokens of a fractionalized asset to a broad investor base requires the presentation of sensitive property data in a very public manner, raising the question of data confidentiality.

Some experts have, additionally, questioned whether there truly is demand for fractionalized and tokenized real estate, especially when considering that most of the promised benefits cannot yet be realized. The lack of demand could, however, simply stem from a lack of education on tokenization in real estate and generally on the underlying blockchain technology. Education is considered essential to establish trust and an understanding for both the potential and risks of tokenized assets. The lack of demand could likewise stem from the missing exit strategies for token investments. As long as a secondary market exchange is missing, investors might be hesitant about buying tokens.

6.3 RQ3: Case Studies and Expert Interviews: What Are the Current Best Practices and Lessons Learnt?

RQ1 and RQ2 have shown that while there are large theoretical advantages to implementing blockchain and tokenization in real estate, the solutions must also be judged for use cases as the implementation can look different in practice. In Switzerland, there are three use cases where properties have successfully been tokenized. Hello World by blockimmo, Bahnhofstrasse 52 (B52) by BrickMark, and then two properties that make up the Crowdlitoken portfolio. The Hello World property was tokenized to 20% on the Ethereum blockchain, and the equity tokens were sold to four investors in a club deal in exchange for CryptoFranc. The investors each hold a contract with the seller establishing the ownership rights as the tokens themselves do not carry any legal weight. B52 was purchased by BrickMark from RFR Holdings and 20% of the purchase price was paid for with BrickMark Tokens (BMT). The BMT is a hybrid security token based on the Ethereum blockchain with an ERC-20 token standard and has not (yet) been listed. The two properties in the Crowdlitoken portfolio were acquired following a financing round where CHF 16 million worth of CRTs were issued and sold to around 450 investors. The underlying subordinate bonds were issued at a minimum return of 0.825% in years 1 and 2, 1.4875% in year 3, and 2.1% from year 4 and onwards with a 25-year term until

December 14, 2044. CRTs and the two properties of the Crowdlitoken portfolio are still open for investment at a minimum investment amount of CHF 100.

In short, for all three case studies, the tokenization was carried out differently even though all three companies were founded with the same fundamental reasoning and idea. For each case study, the respective interview partners described the difficulty of carrying out the tokenization of a real estate asset early on, and how things had to be done on a trial-and-error basis. They all had to go through the processes of figuring out what intermediate structure could work, what exactly should be tokenized, how to best set up the blockchain, code the smart contracts, align the transaction or set up the investment platform, and then convince potential investors of the investment opportunity. Throughout this process, the lack of regulatory guidelines was of particular concern as it was not yet clear what requirements had to be met. As a result, expectations had to be adjusted and compromises be made. In the case of Hello World, for example, it was not thousands of different investors partaking in the project but four, still, the transaction could successfully be carried out via blockchain and without any intermediaries. Meanwhile, Crowdlitoken had a successful first financing round, however, onboarding new investors has proven to be challenging and is limiting the growth of the portfolio.

Analysing the statements of the interviews did not reveal one best practice to tokenize a real estate asset. However, with the addition of the DLT Act and the presence of use cases in the market, the experts agree that tokenization has become easier. Rind stated that tokenizing debt (usually in the form of a bond) is currently the easiest method. According to Don, however, the tokenization of equity in the form of tokenizing company shares should be preferred as it provides better investor security. Meanwhile, Dr. Luchsinger specified that a real estate company for qualified investors would be the simplest intermediate structure to set up but comes with limitations. One aspect which was mentioned for all three case studies was the need for education on the topics of blockchain, tokenization, and digital assets as well as the subsequent investment opportunities. Hereby, the interfaces which are needed to access these opportunities should be adapted to be more user-friendly. Finally, the interviewees all stated the need for a secondary market exchange to offer investors an exit strategy, reinforcing the results of the secondary research. In relation to this, Don and Dr. Luchsinger agreed that the SIX Digital Exchange (SDX) is not the blockchain-based decentralized peer-to-peer exchange that market participants had hoped for.

While the experts recognize that their endeavours might have been too innovative too soon, they all experienced large interest in their projects from a variety of market participants and are convinced that their pioneering work within the tokenization of real estate sent a strong message. Consequently, all interview partners still see large potential in especially the blockchain technology itself coupled with smart contracts, but also in its application within the real estate token industry. They agree that the market has developed positively on a global level, and specifically in Switzerland with the DLT Act offering increased legal security. Don, however, pointed out that development within the Swiss market did not change significantly following the DLT Act. Still, the interview partners concluded that it is a question of when a broader implementation of blockchain and tokenization will be seen in the real estate market and not if.

Unsurprisingly, all interview partners are still active in the real estate token market even if some of the case studies lie a few years back. Don from blockimmo renamed and re-positioned the company to Token Factory, acting as a technology provider and consultant for tokenization projects. They also shifted their focus from Swiss real estate properties to Eastern European real estate portfolios and are still working on the STX.SWISS exchange. Since the tokenization of B52, Rind has founded BrickGate aiming to become the biggest marketplace for real estate-backed tokens in Europe. With BrickGate Rind wants to offer a platform and be a provider for all services needed for the tokenization of real estate assets. Meanwhile, the Crowdlitoken portfolio is still open for investments. While an alternative way of financing could be in the works according to Büchi, Crowdlitoken is currently not looking to add new properties as there is still capacity for investments in the two existing ones.

6.4 RQ4: What Recommendations Can Be Given to Different Market Participants Going Forward?

To answer RQ4 and be able to compose suitable recommendations to market participants, it is first necessary to establish where the market should be heading, meaning, what implementations of blockchain and tokens within the real estate industry make sense and are beneficial to the market? This is necessary, as it is not yet apparent how and to which extent tokenization will be implemented and, as a result, will impact and shape the market.

The implementation of a blockchain as an alternative for storing property data and/or valuations seems to come with many advantages. Assuming the technology works well, it could greatly improve data transparency and administrative efforts and, as a result, save time and costs throughout real estate management, investment, and transaction processes. Applying blockchain technology to tokenize and potentially fractionalize a real estate asset also holds, in theory, many benefits. In practice, however, there are limiting factors that hinder market participants from realizing these benefits. These include the land register, regulatory uncertainties, and the lack of a secondary market exchange. The latter is especially important as without it, real estate tokens will be just as illiquid as their traditional counterparts and many of the potential benefits of tokenization can't be harvested.

In terms of the regulatory framework, it has been established that the direct tokenization and fractionalization of a real estate asset is currently not possible, and instead, intermediate structures are used. However, the indirect tokenization of a real estate asset does likewise not allow for the full realization of the potential benefits, it adds to the complexity of the investment opportunity which can decrease efficiency and increase costs. Consequently, some researchers have questioned the currently attainable value-adding element of tokenization. On the other hand, some researchers have stated that the current use cases are a good way to familiarize the market with the concept and in turn facilitate further development. Still, the question arises whether such structures are in line with the original idea of a decentralized real estate investment opportunity? This question also applies to a potentially suitable secondary market exchange, as an entirely decentralized exchange is not yet possible in Switzerland due to regulations requiring trading facilities to be operated by a Swiss entity. In contrast, one could discuss whether the token infrastructure needs to be entirely decentralized and whether that is even realistic?

Another aspect to consider is the uncertainty around demand from investors for tokenized and fractionalized real estate assets. Baum questions this in their extensive research, and, amongst other things, argues that real estate crowdfunding so far has seen little success. Other research and the presented case studies suggest the same challenge. A common explanation is the general lack of awareness and knowledge around blockchain technology and tokenization, concerns regarding security and volatility of digital assets, as well as the lack of a secondary market exchange. However, assuming investors get educated and trust the investment opportunities, a secondary market is available, and the tokenization and fractionalization of real estate assets is possible, the question of demand remains. How involved do retail investors want to be in their investment decisions? Do they want to be able to pick each individual investment? Currently, most retail investors will participate in a fund and/or have a bank take care of their investments. Will that change with the addition of new digital investment opportunities or will real estate tokens simply become a diversification tool for funds from which retail investors benefit indirectly? One could also argue that even if many don't take direct advantage of such investment opportunities they should still exist for the sake of democratizing the real estate asset class. However, without adequate demand will there be an incentive to create supply?

In conclusion, researchers have questioned whether blockchain is truly a disruptor of the market or whether it simply offers a new foundational technology on which the market can work. While the potential benefits of tokenization are clear and have been reviewed many times, there are obviously still many challenges to overcome and questions to be answered. Blockchain and tokenization will not solve all problems in the industry. Nevertheless, a review of the development of both technical solutions and services and of regulatory certainty around the world showcased how quickly the market is currently moving. Interest in blockchain-based solutions and products is still increasing and governments and politicians are pressured to act accordingly. As a result, experts are confident that it is a question of when and not if a wide adoption will be seen in the market. Hereby, the respective timeline will largely depend on how quickly the different countries can outline the necessary regulatory framework. So, while current implementations cannot (yet) offer the promised benefits and the manner of future implementations is uncertain, many participants are convinced of the potential and want to move towards a broader adoption. Overarching recommendations could help facilitate and streamline development, so the theoretical benefits can be realized as fully as possible.

Assuming that the overall market would like to push the implementation of blockchain and tokenization within the real estate market, having understood the potential opportunities and challenges, there are some key aspects to consider. First and foremost, the importance of cooperation should be highlighted. Experts and market players agree that a communal effort will be necessary to further push development and enable a wider adoption that can harvest the full potential that blockchain and tokenization hold. Such cooperation is especially important when aiming for an interoperable infrastructure that can allow for real estate investments and transactions to be carried out across different blockchains and borders. It also includes considering the protection of investors, particularly new retail investors.

Within this cooperation, the different market players have different roles and tasks to fulfil. Legislators, for example, will need to ensure clear guidelines and regulations around the implementation of blockchain and tokenization. Meanwhile, the government would, ideally, provide a digitalized solution for the land register and research blockchain solutions for the management of an array of different data. Throughout these processes, political support for the increased adoption of blockchain and tokenization will be necessary. Still, private companies should consider the pros and cons of implementing a blockchain solution. When deciding to do so, regulatory and technical elements need to be carefully analysed to create an adequate set-up while adhering to legal guidelines. At the same time, the market should find a way to agree on technical standards to ensure that blockchains are interoperable.

Having said that, the potential lack of demand has been noted multiple times and needs to be addressed. Consequently, the creation of a secondary market exchange should be a priority of market participants. Furthermore, initiatives to educate the broader market on the opportunities and risks of real estate token investment should be launched. In the meantime, retail investors are recommended to simply become more familiar with the technology and concept and explore some of the already available solutions and offers for digital assets. Generally, the market should also watch out for players that are taking advantage of the current hype, feel pressured to appear progressive and implement new technological solutions but with minimal effort and resources, and/or players which claim to be working with blockchain when they aren't.

Finally, the real estate market is a well-coordinated interaction of market players who have all found a way to benefit from the current set-up. While most would benefit from the above-described cooperative effort to implement blockchain (increased efficiency and transparency, decreasing costs and time) and tokenization (better access to capital and increased liquidity), some might also experience negative effects (their role within the market might diminish, they can't take advantage of information asymmetry, there are new alternatives to, e.g., take a loan). For these market players, research generally recommends reviewing and possibly adapting their services and products to fit the new environment. This could entail leaving task-based elements to be handled by the technology while adding value through consultancy-based work. Should the implementation of blockchain and tokenization be successful on a wide scale, as many experts predict, some players might struggle to find their place within the market if they have failed to adapt to the new structure. It is, therefore, recommendable to at least keep tabs on market developments.

Chapter 7
Summary and Outlook

Following the conclusion, this final chapter will summarize the results of this research paper including listing the recommendations to market participants. Furthermore, a critical reflection of the work and an outlook for further research in the field of tokenization in real estate are presented.

7.1 Summary

The common drawbacks of real estate as an asset class are clear: a traditional real estate transaction requires multiple intermediaries such as a bank, notary, and agent as well as considerable administrative efforts. Also, the average due diligence process can be time-consuming as property and market data often lack transparency. Meanwhile, most transactions are carried out in private markets, omitting a large pool of potential investors. At the same time, the average investor has a hard time directly accessing the asset class due to high capital requirements and because only around 10% of the market is available through standard investment vehicles. As a result of these factors, traditional real estate investment is considered illiquid, inaccessible, and untransparent while transactions are costly and time- consuming. Tokenization promises to overcome many of these shortcomings.

Tokenization in real estate can refer to both the digital representation of a real estate asset and the digital representation of ownership of a real estate asset. Tokenization often also implies the fractionalization of said ownership rights. Both are enabled through the utilization of blockchain technology and usually also smart contracts. Tokenization in real estate offers a range of opportunities and benefits. Especially, if the asset is not only tokenized but also fractionalized. The main advantages include increased liquidity, new sources of capital, and democratizing the asset class as entry barriers are lowered. Furthermore, data transparency and in turn security are associated with the implementation of blockchain technology, while

E. Schmid et al., *Tokenization in Real Estate*, SpringerBriefs in Finance, https://doi.org/10.1007/978-3-031-55810-8_7

smart contracts can facilitate the automation of tasks. All together the tokenization and fractionalization of real estate assets based on blockchain technology and smart contracts can allow for significant increases in efficiency and decreases in cost throughout real estate investment and transaction processes.

In practice, there are a series of challenges hindering the full realization of these benefits. Most importantly, the regulatory framework needs to be discussed. While regulations can be considered well- developed in international comparison, an analysis of the current legal situation in Switzerland including an interview with legal expert Dr. Luchsinger showed that there are still uncertainties around the requirements for digital securities. Furthermore, the current regulations prevent the direct tokenization and fractionalization of real estate assets. Consequently, issuers of real estate tokens must add an intermediate structure to hold the asset. Instead of the asset itself, the intermediate structure is tokenized and fractionalized. This adds to the complexity and, as a result, can again decrease efficiency and entail additional costs. A further aspect limiting the development of tokenization in real estate is the potential lack of demand for fractionalized real estate investment opportunities. This lack of demand could, however, simply stem from a lack of education, understanding and trust of tokenization and blockchain technology. Likewise, the missing exit strategy for token investments could be building hesitation among market participants towards investing in these new digital securities. Still, these factors raise the question of the currently attainable value-adding element of tokenization. Most of the promised benefits cannot (yet) be realized and for the industry to move towards blockchain and tokenization, evident advantages over traditional market processes need to be achievable.

Having reviewed the theoretical concept of tokenization, its application, opportunities, and challenges, use cases were analysed to complete the research. There are three use cases of tokenized real estate assets in Switzerland. These were approached in the form of case studies including expert interviews with the founders or representatives of management of the respective companies. The case studies illustrated that the implementation of tokenization can look different in practice. Different from each other, as they all chose their individual legal and technical setup but also different from the theoretical exemplary idea of the concept of tokenization in real estate. The analysis of the three case studies did not clearly reveal any one best practice for tokenizing a real estate asset in Switzerland. However, the interviewees stated that the process of tokenization has become simpler, and the market environment has evolved positively, especially also due to increased regulatory certainty provided by the DLT Act. The interviewees further reinforced many of the results of the secondary research by, for example, stating the lack of knowledge and trust of market participants and the need for a secondary market exchange. Overall, all three companies were early in entering this new market and sometimes had to struggle to find their way. Still, the interviewees were convinced that their achievements sent a strong message to the market and concluded that it is not a question of if a broader implementation of blockchain and tokenization will be seen but when. Unsurprisingly, all interview partners are still active in the real estate token market, even if some have adjusted their business model in the meantime.

In contrast to companies like blockimmo, BrickMark, or Crowdlitoken there are market players which have actively built business models around the illiquidity and information asymmetry of the traditional real estate market. In fact, when reviewing the current market situation in Switzerland, it becomes apparent that it is a well-coordinated interaction of market players who have all found a way to benefit from the current set-up. Consequently, not everyone might be excited about blockchain technology and tokenization. Limited support or even pushback could be expected from these parties. Similarly, political opposition could come into play, as tokenization might further increase property prices. However, when reviewing current developments within the market a strong interest and evolvement of products, services, and regulations can be observed, also on an international level. Many participants seem to be convinced of the potential of tokenization in real estate and want to move towards a wider adoption. Should they be successful, participants who fail to adapt could struggle to remain relevant within the market.

In conclusion, blockchain technology and tokenization are not the solution to everything. Products and businesses are not automatically better because a blockchain has been implemented and an asset has been tokenized—the underlying property still needs to be a good investment. Consequently, any implementation should be reviewed carefully for its feasible benefits and risks. Nevertheless, the potential that blockchain technology and tokenization hold are significant. Within the real estate market, both are in their early stages of development and implementation, and it is simply not yet clear what their future role and impact will be. While there have only been a few use cases in Switzerland, the market environment is favourable and many market participants are convinced of the concept and keep pushing for continued development. It can, therefore, be assumed that blockchain and tokenization in real estate are here to stay. If some of the key challenges such as the lack of a secondary market exchange and the limited knowledge and trust of market participants can be addressed, there should be well-suited areas for its wider application.

The discussed recommendations to market participants to facilitate the wider adoption of tokenization in real estate, aiming to realize the potential benefits as effectively as possible, can be divided into two categories. First, recommendations for the general market environment, to create and ensure the ideal underlying market conditions. Then, the recommendations to market participants active within that environment. The recommendations are summarized below.

Recommendations for the market environment:

- *Cooperation*: Generally, cooperation between different entities and market participants should be pursued to ensure a wider adoption can harvest the full potential that blockchain and tokenization hold.
- *Regulatory Framework*: Legislators should ensure legal certainty and security around the implementation of blockchain solutions, tokenization, and digital securities.
- *Land Register*: Ideally, the government would provide a digitalized land register solution.

- *Education*: Initiatives to educate the wider market on real estate token investments, including the potential benefits and risks, should be composed to increase trust amongst market participants. Meanwhile, participants are encouraged to explore the sphere of digital assets.
- *Secondary Market Exchange*: The availability of a secondary market exchange will be key in the wider adoption of tokenization in real estate. Allowing for its creation should, therefore, be a priority of market participants.

Recommendations to market participants:

- *Tokenization*: Continued testing with blockchain technology and tokenization in real estate is encouraged as it will support development and, therefore, a wider adoption. Nevertheless, tokenizing a real estate asset should be considered carefully, including reviewing the potential opportunities as well as challenges.
- *Implementation*: When implementing a blockchain and tokenizing a real estate asset, different legal structures and jurisdictions with their respective regulatory frameworks as well as different technical solutions should be reviewed, including their advantages and disadvantages. By that, an adequate set-up can be created which is suited to the individual situation.
- *Interoperability*: Market participants should aim to establish technical standards to ensure the interoperability of different blockchains.
- *Investors*: Investors should review the real estate token market for its investment opportunities. Hereby, investors are recommended to consider both the potential upsides and the potential risks of such opportunities.
- *Adapting Business Models*: Providers currently active in the real estate field should review their business models to identify how they could potentially adapt to a wider adoption of tokenization. Additionally, the development of tokenization in real estate should be followed closely to avoid falling behind and being rendered irrelevant in the market.

7.2 Critical Reflection

An inductive exploratory study was carried out to thoroughly understand the concept as well as the current market situation of tokenization in real estate. First and foremost, the research shows that tokenization in real estate is still in its very beginnings and its future role in the market is not yet apparent. Consequently, the results of this study cannot be considered definite and there are still questions to be answered. Furthermore, the paper only presents a snapshot of the current real estate token market. Developments and changes within the market happen continuously, shaping the described opportunities and challenges. Adjustments to the above-presented recommendations might, therefore, be necessary down the line. Additionally, this research has mostly focused on the situation in Switzerland and only a brief international review was included. However, in terms of market developments and regulatory frameworks, large differences can be observed between jurisdictions. As a result, market recommendations for countries other than Switzerland might need to be adapted to fit their individual situation.

Among academics, the topic of tokenization in real estate is likewise considered novel. As a result, the availability of academic research on the topic is limited, especially as research naturally lags behind the market development. The secondary research, therefore, included many sources outside of academic research. At the same time, the overarching topics of blockchain and blockchain applications including cryptocurrencies, for example, have grown to be immense. Here, clear boundaries had to be set and the comparably narrow topic of tokenization in real estate remained in focus but was instead analysed thoroughly. In addition, the underlying technical aspects of tokenization were not reviewed in detail. In terms of primary research, which focused on analysing use cases in Switzerland, only three cases of tokenized real estate assets can be found in Switzerland. While, therefore, the entirety of the market could be covered, it also limits the significance of the analysis and the results.

7.3 Further Research

Tokenization in real estate is a new but dynamic concept and developments in the market are happening continuously. Researchers in the field should, therefore, keep observing the market's evolvement and add to the currently limited research on the topic. Especially as the market is still in its very beginnings, significant changes can be expected. Overall, further research will very much depend on the direction that tokenization will take in the real estate market, including aspects of the underlying market environment such as regulatory changes, technological possibilities, and the success or failure of future use cases.

Following the key results, some specific areas of research within the topic are suggested. The cooperation among market participants and the availability of a secondary market exchange as well as the technical interoperability of blockchains with applicable standards are key for a wider adoption. Targeted research on these aspects could offer the market helpful guidelines and support. Also, more in-depth research on the regulatory framework in Switzerland could provide legislators with a summary of current uncertainties as well as potential adjustments to facilitate a wider adoption. Similarly, research on the digitalization of the land register could provide administrations with guidance on the technical components as well as on the form and content of such a platform. Additional research could further focus on determining efficient solutions to educating market participants on real estate token investments to increase understanding, trust, and demand. Finally, after some time, the situation in the market including new use cases should be reviewed again. Ideally, the market will have matured and best practices can be determined. Then, a legitimate comparison between traditional and tokenized real estate investments could be made, revealing which parts of the potential of tokenization are feasible.

The research and subsequent conclusion also revealed some unanswered questions, proposing a basis for further research. Specifically, the needs and wants of retail investors concerning their personal investments could be analysed to uncover whether there truly is a lack of demand for tokenized and fractionalized real estate investment opportunities and if so, why. Furthermore, the topic of decentralization could be reviewed further. How decentralized can and should the token economy and the various parts of its infrastructure be? What are the advantages and disadvantages of different levels of decentralization?

Appendix A Interview Guides

E. Schmid et al., *Tokenization in Real Estate*, SpringerBriefs in Finance,
https://doi.org/10.1007/978-3-031-55810-8

Interview Guide – Master Thesis
Tokenization in Real Estate

HSLU Hochschule Luzern

Interview Guide – Master Thesis

Interviewer: ....

Interviewee, Company: ....

Date, Location: ....

Introduction

Research Aim: Establish an overview of tokenization in real estate (technical, legal & current market situation). Form recommendations for market participants to broaden the application of tokenization in real estate (in Switzerland), based on secondary research and case studies.
Structure of Interview: Semi-structured interview with a guide for orientation. All information will be solely used for the purpose of this master thesis. The interview will last approximately 1 hour.

Interview

1. Background

Tell me about your background, what inspired/motivated you to work with the tokenization of real estate?

2. Company-specific

Tell me about your company. What is your purpose/are your main goals? Why have you chosen to move from traditional real estate (investment) to blockchain?

3. Case-specific

3.1 Tell me about the tokenized asset(s), what have you achieved so far and how?
3.2 What elements were most important to successfully carry out the tokenization of an asset?
3.3 What were the biggest challenges you encountered?
3.4 What are your lessons learnt/what will you do differently with the next asset?
3.5 What was the interest of your investors and how was the perception? Is there a demand for fractionalized and tokenized assets?

4. Personal Opinions & Recommendations

4.1 In your opinion, what are the current best practices for tokenizing real estate in the Swiss market?
4.2 What are your (specific) recommendations to the various market participants (investors, owners, legislators) going forward for successfully broadening the application of tokenization in the Swiss real estate market? OR What do the various market participants need to do, to take advantage of Switzerland being amongst the first movers?
4.3 What is your opinion on the future development of tokenization in real estate in Switzerland? What are the main "competing" countries?
4.4 What is your opinion on trends and the future development of tokenization in real estate on a global level?

5. Final Question

Do you have a final comment/advisement to add?

Conclusion

Summary: Review of the points discussed.
Further Steps: Would you like to receive the final paper?

Thank you!

Interview Guide – Master Thesis
Tokenization in Real Estate

HSLU Hochschule Luzern

Interview Guide – Master Thesis

Interviewer: ....

Interviewee, Company: ....

Date, Location: ....

Introduction

Research Aim: Establish an overview of tokenization in real estate (technical, legal & current market situation). Form recommendations for market participants to broaden the application of tokenization in real estate (in Switzerland), based on secondary research and case studies.
Structure of Interview: Semi-structured interview with a guide for orientation. All information will be solely used for the purpose of this master thesis. The interview will last approximately 1 hour.

Interview

1. Background

Tell me about your background, what inspired/motivated you to work with the tokenization of real estate?

2. Legal Foundations in CH

2.1 What are the current legal foundations in Switzerland which need to be taken into account when discussing the tokenization of real estate assets?
2.2 Switzerland is said to be among the first movers within the tokenization of real estate assets, why (key elements)? How can we maintain and take advantage of this position?
2.3 Which are, in your opinion, the biggest legal challenges going forward when aiming to broaden the application of real estate tokens in Switzerland.

3. Personal Opinions & Recommendations

3.1 In your opinion, what are the current best practices for tokenizing real estate in the Swiss market?
3.2 What are your (specific) recommendations to the various market participants (investors, owners, legislators) going forward for successfully broadening the application of tokenization in the Swiss real estate market? OR What do the various market participants need to do, to take advantage of Switzerland being amongst the first movers?
3.3 What is your opinion on the future development of tokenization in real estate in Switzerland? Where do you see potential for investments via tokens?
3.4 What is your opinion on trends and the future development of tokenization in real estate on a global level? What are the main "competing" countries?

4. Final Question

Do you have a final comment/advisement to add?

Conclusion

Summary: Review of the points discussed.
Further Steps: Would you like to receive the final paper?

Thank you!

Appendix B Interview Transcript Dr. Luchsinger

E. Schmid et al., *Tokenization in Real Estate*, SpringerBriefs in Finance, https://doi.org/10.1007/978-3-031-55810-8

Interview Guide – Master Thesis
Tokenization in Real Estate

HSLU Hochschule Luzern

Interview Guide – Master Thesis

Interviewer: Elena Schmid...

Interviewee, Company: Dr. Catrina Luchsinger, MLL...

Date, Location: 04.05.2022, Zürich...

Introduction

Research Aim: Establish an overview of tokenization in real estate (technical, legal & current market situation). Form recommendations for market participants to broaden the application of tokenization in real estate (in Switzerland), based on secondary research and case studies.
Structure of Interview: Semi-structured interview with a guide for orientation. All information will be solely used for the purpose of this master thesis. The interview will last approximately 1 hour.

Interview

1. Background

Tell me about your background, what inspired/motivated you to work with the tokenization of real estate?

2. Legal Foundations in CH

2.1 What are the current legal foundations in Switzerland which need to be taken into account when discussing the tokenization of real estate assets?

- *The economic model/structure (fund, KAG, Immobiliengesellschaft, equity, debt, etc.) and taxes. Then it depends on where the issuers are situated, the assets and where investors are from (where will the tokens be distributed to). These elements determine which jurisdictions and which regulations apply. You really need to consider all factors and find individual solutions to create the most advantageous structure.*
- *There are some regulatory and taxation elements which have not yet been solved, e.g., the "Gewinnbesteuerung", indicating that direct tokenization might still take some time. Another element which is slowing down development is Lex Koller, as it limits the distribution of residential real estate tokens abroad.*

2.2 Switzerland is said to be among the first movers within the tokenization of real estate assets, why (key elements)? How can we maintain and take advantage of this position?

- *Regulatory security/certainty ("Regulierungssicherheit"): Swiss law has defined what a token is and what a token does/can do. The FINMA ensured this security early on. So far, for regulatory gaps, they have usually observed the market for a bit but then come in quite early to make decisions and set regulations.*
- *Furthermore, Switzerland also has very good and knowledgeable consultants, within the law, tech., tax, etc. supporting companies in implementing these new solutions.*
- *However, even these experts cannot with absolute certainty answer all questions, this is often the case for new laws. In such cases, a 'non-action letter' offers the possibility to contact FINMA, describe the situation and suggest a solution. The FINMA can then agree or disagree with the proposed solution. This will delay the advancement of a project but it offers additional security. Currently, there are more open questions within the field of DeFi as opposed to in real estate.*

2.3 Which are, in your opinion, the biggest legal challenges going forward when aiming to broaden the application of real estate tokens in Switzerland.

- *Blockchain should start to find its way into administrations ("Verwaltungen"), e.g., digitalize the register for car plates/car numbers. However, Switzerland is working very slowly towards such updates, just as with the E-ID.*
- *A digital identity on a blockchain is needed. There is enough trust in the Swiss government for them to create a permissioned blockchain which could hold personal data: health care, real estate, ID, etc. Ideally, all this data would exist on one connected infrastructure.*
- *Currently, blockchain infrastructure such as the crypto world is highly fragmented, making it very difficult to develop it further. Also, the available user interfaces are not designed for a broad application. People are worried about cyber security, there is a lack of understanding for blockchain technology and for crypto. It will, therefore, still be a long time until "Herr und Frau Schweizer" have their real estate asset/their home on a blockchain. For that to happen the user interface needs to be designed in an easy and intuitive manner.*
    - *Example 1: you sit down on a chair, you don't question whether it will 'work', meaning whether it will hold you, and this doesn't change if the design of the chair differs. The same principle should work for a digitalized data infrastructure – you shouldn't question how it works/what technology lies behind it, you should be judging the user interface.*
    - *Example 2: when comparing an iPhone with an Android you don't take them apart to check the technology, you judge them by how user friendly they are. However, for blockchain, the IT due diligence is, currently, one of the most important steps.*
- *In short, you should be able to login into your commune's network and have access to all your personal data with a user-friendly interface, not questioning what technology is making it possible. However, there is a jungle of different blockchain standards available and many are not trustworthy (hence the need for an IT due diligence). Finding a good, trustworthy project within all the created blockchains will take years.*
- *Creating such a national data infrastructure will not happen all at once, it's going to happen in small baby steps as people will increasingly use and rely upon the technology and pressure upon the government to implement it more increases.*
- *Some cantons have already started to work with a blockchain, however, they are often not cooperating with each other. Meaning, they are not applying the same standards and might, e.g., work with a different login, making it very difficult to build an API which could work with all of these different systems. A nation-wide/governmental approach/project is necessary to unify the application, and such an approach will start with the E-ID.*

Within tokenization there are two steps:

1. *You use the economic benefit which can be extracted from e.g., a real estate asset and tokenize it.*
2. *You tokenize the asset itself. However, for this to work you need to digitalize an array of data first. If Switzerland truly wants to be at the forefront and e.g., be able to comfortably hold discussions with the EU, not needing to join them as they are strong enough, a nation-wide digital infrastructure project could be the foundation to create and secure such a position.*

4. Personal Opinions & Recommendations

4.1 In your opinion, what are the current best practices for tokenizing real estate in the Swiss market?

- *In terms of economic models, Dr. Luchsiner does not have a favorite, but believes there is a good solution for every project. When tokenization starts to become a norm, there will be multiple solutions for issuers to choose from. It then depends on the prerequisites and what they are more comfortable with.*
- *However, the easiest form would be a "Immobiliengesellschaft für qualifizierte Anleger". This structure does have some disadvantages as the tokens couldn't be freely distributed or traded. To remove this limitation a "Immobiliengesellschaft für nicht qualifizierte Anleger" could need be created, requiring the company to be listed at the SDX.*

Interview Guide – Master Thesis
Tokenization in Real Estate

HSLU Hochschule Luzern

- *SDX is not really a blockchain application, it does not enable peer-to-peer transactions, behind the scenes there are still banks and traditional processes in place. It was not the solution, which many hoped for, and did, therefore, not create an exuberant reaction.*

4.2 What are your (specific) recommendations to the various market participants (investors, owners, legislators) going forward for successfully broadening the application of tokenization in the Swiss real estate market? OR What do the various market participants need to do, to take advantage of Switzerland being amongst the first movers?

- *Market participants should now start, privately but also within their jobs, to work with different crypto and token applications, follow developments and start to understand these concepts.*
- *The curiosity for these topics, which began in 2015/16, should also start to move into the corporate world. People will increasingly come into touch with crypto and blockchain and start to use/implement it, so should companies.*
- *Dr. Luchsinger can well imagine e.g., a pension fund with a new, smaller-scaled structured product based on crypto. Corporations/entities should be open to go new ways and communicate with regulators to find out what is possible.*

4.3 What is your opinion on the future development of tokenization in real estate in Switzerland? Where do you see potential for investments via tokens?

- *Dr. Luchsinger's vision is that more and more shares from new companies are issued as "Registerwertrechte", allowing the new corporate generation to grow up with tokens which you can directly hold in your wallet without needing a custodian. It is a generational question; the older generation has less touch points with blockchain while for the younger generation tokens will become a norm.*
- *There will also be new products to aggregate tokens. Meaning a wallet which can hold all of your tokens. Right now, you can't hold all your crypto assets and tokens in the same wallet due to different technical standards. You also need different exchanges compared to fiat currencies where you can change most currencies at any one exchange.*
- *How can we come from this extreme diversity in services to a more structures and organized infrastructure? Likely with a more centralized solution offered by a crypto bank. There are many organizations trying to find solutions to this problem, and to other issues as well, e.g., inheritance – if something happens to you, what happens to your digital assets? How can I trade these assets, how can I exit the investment? etc.*
- *Competition to offer good cheap technical solutions for such an aggregated platform will be strong. In terms of creating a secondary market, it might be easier task for some asset classes than others, as some assets have rigid frameworks and requirements for transactions which would still need to be respected even if tokenized. Still tokenization could ease the administrative effort and any technical improvement/digitalization to simplify (administrative) processes are a step into the right direction.*

4.4 What is your opinion on trends and the future development of tokenization in real estate on a global level? What are the main "competing" countries?

- *Real estate specifically, is a very national market, even with tokenization you will still need a local expert, so competition is less of a discussion.*
- *Overall, Liechtenstein is a competitor. Digital assets/crypto assets are well regulated, they are flexible, and regulators are easy to contact. In the Asian market, Singapore (even though it has been quiet for a bit) is also further along.*
- *In terms of financial products, the US is strong. American banks can give out tokenized derivatives, stable coins, etc. without being limited by regulators. Switzerland is, in fact, more generous with the distribution of such products in Switzerland than with the creation as developing the necessary infrastructure would be subject to approval while participation is not.*

5. Final Question

Do you have a final comment/advisement to add?

- *The different economic structures, what is possible and for whom, should be reviewed further.*
- *Similarly, direct asset tokenization and the link to the necessity of a basic data structure starting with an E-ID should be reviewed.*
- *Also, an exchange which is truly a token exchange will be necessary. A better alternative to SDX. A peer-to-peer exchange where tokens are traded, using whitelisting for verified investors. Japan has the goal to create such a digital exchange for securities by the end of the year. This would truly be a game changer: an approved, peer-to-peer network in a secure jurisdiction.*

Conclusion

Summary: Review of the points discussed.
Further Steps: Would you like to receive the final paper? **Yes.**

Thank you!

Appendix C Interview Transcript Bastiaan Don (Hello World)

E. Schmid et al., *Tokenization in Real Estate*, SpringerBriefs in Finance,
https://doi.org/10.1007/978-3-031-55810-8

HSLU Hochschule Luzern

Interview Guide – Master Thesis

Interviewer: Elena Schmid...

Interviewee, Company: Bastiaan Don, blockimmo..

Date, Location: 11.04.2022, Bern (Zoom)..

Introduction

Research Aim: Establish an overview of tokenization in real estate (technical, legal & current market situation). Form recommendations for market participants to broaden the application of tokenization in real estate (in Switzerland), based on secondary research and case studies.
Structure of Interview: Semi-structured interview with a guide for orientation. All information will be solely used for the purpose of this master thesis. The interview will last approximately 1 hour.

Interview

1. Background

Tell me about your background, what inspired/motivated you to work with the tokenization of real estate?

- *Don has always been very IT interested, started to program and develop websites. Even founded a company during their studies with a friend, renting out furnished apartments to expats on the internet in 2006. Everything was carried out online, and they developed the software themselves.*
- *As a result, they got a lot of experience within the real estate market, in property management, refurbishments, construction site management, and real estate transactions.*
- *Then discovered bitcoin and the underlying technology blockchain.*
- *Don then thought about combining blockchain and real estate in around 2018 and founded blockimmo as they saw a lot of potential.*

2. Company-specific

Tell me about your company. What is your purpose/are your main goals? Why have you chosen to move from traditional real estate (investment) to blockchain?

blockimmo:

- *In 2018, blockimmo was able to start right away with a potential project. They ended up fulfilling a pioneering role with the project. Throughout the process, they aimed to build a product which was tangible, and they did everything in-house.*
- *The goal, initially, was to demonstrate that blockchain can be applied in a regulated market (or in a market where securities are regulated) and be compliant with said regulations without giving up on decentralization. The overall goal was, also, to enable anyone to invest in real estate and give anyone access to this investment class. Moreover, it provided real estate owners with another capital markets for liquidity. Finally, blockimmo wanted to create a secondary market for the fractionalized shares of real estate with their project STX.SWISS.*
- *The move away from traditional real estate investment was also due to Don's own experience. When wanting to sell a property in Switzerland you have a list of maybe 20, 50 or 100 potential buyers, of which you know many on a personal level. The deals are then often carried out behind closed doors. It is a well working system but dominated by very few companies and family-offices. It doesn't result in many interesting investments opportunities.*

Token Factory:

- *Throughout the first tokenization project, blockimmo was also talking to other potential owners. However, by the time they had educated them on the technology and built-up trust, they had already sold their properties, in a traditional manner, to other investors. That in combination with other challenges encountered during the first project, moved blockimmo to re-name and re-position themselves. They have moved away from Swiss real estate and instead capitalize on their tokenization solution for securities. Today they are known as Token Factory.*
- *Token Factory acts as technology provider and does consultancy for a variety of projects. They, for example, tokenized the first fund in Liechtenstein with Bank Frick, are currently working on a gold-backed project, in the wine industry, etc.*
- *Furthermore, they are still working on STX.SWISS and are in close contact with FINMA to enable decentralized trading for regulated assets.*
- *In terms of real estate, they are currently looking at high-yield properties in Eastern Europe, offering owners to liquidate 10, 20, 30% of their portfolio. The legal structure will most likely still be a fund. They see potential in this strategy as it offers high yields to investors with a safe structure in the background, while owners do not need to sell their properties but can still liquidate a large amount from their assets.*
- *They are basically trying to solve the chicken and the egg story before going back into the development of a platform again. They aim to create a secondary market that has substantial liquidity from day one –so you can invest in real estate with your crypto currency, receive monthly pay-outs and liquidate your investment at any time should you need to.*
- *They can't go really live with their platform until they have approval from FINMA. They did, however, put it online just to create some pressure, but progress is currently slow.*

3. Case-specific

3.1 Tell me about the tokenized asset(s), what have you achieved so far and how?

- *Blockimmo has tokenized one asset so far, 'Hello World' in Zug, Switzerland. A residential building with a restaurant on the ground floor.*
- *Back then, there were many cases of tokenizing bonds, so debt. Which, should things go bad, will be the last to be paid out. They are also a lot less regulated. So, blockimmo wanted to stay on the equity side. They chose a fund structure based in Liechtenstein, as Liechtenstein was ahead of Switzerland at that time, at least from a legal perspective. They had a blockchain law draft ready, which later got executed, and they were also very positive towards start-ups. blockimmo worked very closely with Bank Frick and the FMA, while also communicating with FINMA to demonstrate how everything was being executed.*
- *However, they tokenized only 20% of the property. This was on the one hand to show to owners how you can liquidate only a part of your building should you be in need of money, but also so that there would be no change of ownership. As with a change of ownership the land register comes into play and with it a lot of other tricky questions such as tax.*
- *In this case the owners were a family from Zug and the owners really understood the potential of blockchain and were interested to be involved in a such a transaction. Still, it took a lot of education and convincing. Also, they ended up using a stablecoin as it is less volatile and easier to explain to people.*
- *There were four investors in total, they had to convert their investment into CryptoFranc ahead of the transaction. From a legal perspective, setting up a fund for a single asset didn't make any sense so they had a very basic contract for each of the investors with the owners. The tokens themselves did not hold any legal qualifications and blockimmo needed to provide some security.*
- *Still, the result was far away from what they originally set out to achieve; thousands of investors being able to invest in the same property.*
- *From a technical perspective they wrote a software and set-up the blockimmo platform in a decentralized manner, where people can connect with their wallet. They wrote their own smart contract which has been audited by a third party.*
- *Finally, the transaction went through very smoothly, without any financial parties involved.*

- *However, Don believes it was still way too early for the tokenization of a real estate asset.*

3.2 What elements were most important to successfully carry out the tokenization of an asset?

3.3 What were the biggest challenges you encountered?
- *Huge challenge from a legal perspective, however, rather easy from a technical perspective. Back in 2018 there was no legal definition of a token or of a digital asset, but blockimmo still wanted to give the highest form of protection to the investor.*
- *Also, it was and still is not possible to directly tokenize real estate. Nevertheless, blockimmo wanted to demonstrate that the technology works and that a transaction could be carried out using it.*

3.4 What are your lessons learnt/what will you do differently with the next asset?

3.5 What was the interest of your investors and how was the perception? Is there a demand for fractionalized and tokenized assets?
- *Currently there is little demand, especially due to a missing secondary market. People interested in blockchain and crypto need liquidity, they need to know that they can always sell, no matter what token(s) they acquired.*
- *Therefore, investing in tokenized real estate today means taking on additional (liquidity) risk.*

4. Personal Opinions & Recommendations

4.1 In your opinion, what are the current best practices for tokenizing real estate in the Swiss market?
- *Today, if you want to tokenize real estate, tokenizing a share of a company is the way to go. A company can be listed in the land register. It is controlled by management and its board of directors, which can offer some trust to investors. However, even this structure still comes with a lot of hurdles of corporate law.*
- *A bond is never a good idea. Any experienced investor will have some exposure to debt, but it is a high-risk environment and not ideal for tokenized real estate.*

4.2 What are your (specific) recommendations to the various market participants (investors, owners, legislators) going forward for successfully broadening the application of tokenization in the Swiss real estate market? OR What do the various market participants need to do, to take advantage of Switzerland being amongst the first movers?
- *There are still some puzzle pieces missing for tokenization to move on/develop further. The extension of current security laws and recognition of tokens was just one of them.*
- *One of the reasons why the tokenization of securities hasn't taken off more is because people don't quite understand how it works yet.*
- *Regulation is now slowly catching up with stablecoins. Stablecoins have been growing tremendously without regulation, USDT or USDC for example. Don believes it could really help to have these stablecoins regulated so larger investors will feel comfortable trading with them. However, it could still take a couple of years.*
- *From a Swiss perspective, the land register is an issue as well. As long as only natural or juridical person can hold land (and not a 'technical' person such as a smart contract), another layer in terms of ownership is necessary and only indirect tokenization possible. This is a huge breaking element in the entire digitalization process of assets.*
- *There needs to be a secondary market in Switzerland for regulated digital assets. Only then can we talk about what should be tokenized. Don believes real estate will be one of the last securities to be tokenized.*
- *For utility tokens or cryptocurrencies there is already some traction with Bitcoin Suisse and Crypto Finance largely leading the Swiss market.*
- *And then there is the usability; an Ethereum wallet, for example, is not necessarily easy to handle for the everyday user and not ready yet for mass adoption.*

- *To sum up, the three biggest challenges are the missing secondary market, the land register and the current usability of the infrastructure.*
- *Ultimately, if investing in tokenized real estate becomes as easy as investing in any other token, people might start moving towards it.*

4.3 What is your opinion on the future development of tokenization in real estate in Switzerland?
- *New, up-coming opportunities such as NFTs are driving development and interest. However, Don believes that the tokenization of securities will be one of the last steps.*
- *Currently there are a lot of announcements, partnerships, marketing, etc. happening on the market but there is often not a lot of substance. Many of the current big players are not actually interested in the technology and opportunities to develop further. Still they need to present their own involvement, but will do it with limited, actual actions (e.g., SDX).*
- *There needs to be a big player willing to tokenize their entire portfolio (provided there is a secondary market), who sees the potential of being the first to do so. If you are the first to provide such an interesting investment opportunity, the technological infrastructure, an easy-to-use platform/interface, and secondary market then you are number one and there's no reason to move to a different provider. That's the game plan that people are waiting to happen or trying to make to happen. However, many investors/real estate companies are hesitant to make the step as being the first one also comes with a lot of risk.*
- *Another element is real estate development. Blockchain offers an alternative way of raising capital, with more risk but also more return.*
- *Tokenization itself will become a commodity, like websites. In the early days you paid quite a lot of money for a website and today it is free. Tokenization could be similar.*

4.4 What is your opinion on trends and the future development of tokenization in real estate on a global level? What are the main "competing" countries?
- *The US is making process with e.g., MakerDAO.*
- *The EU MiCA draft around cryptocurrencies and secondary exchanges is not too bad, however, not in force yet. The law is trying to solve the secondary market issue around regulated, digitalized assets – should that work, the EU might suddenly be very attractive.*
- *On the other side there are lots of people scared of blockchain, trying to regulate or ban it.*
- *Main competing countries are, amongst others, the US and Singapore.*

5. Final Question

Do you have a final comment/advisement to add?
- *Wants to underline the difference between a real blockchain and everything else which is just trying to ride the wave. The fact that a blockchain can't be controlled by a centralized entity/entities is the core fundament of blockchain. So, if at the end of the day, a hand full of banks or countries are controlling a certain blockchain infrastructure which won the race then we haven't really achieved what we wanted to.*
- *Again, it might work similarly to the internet. In the early days your provider would only allow you to access certain websites. After a while, people were dissatisfied as they couldn't access everything they wanted. For blockchain it might be the same, a semi-centralized solution at the beginning might be helpful to introduce the technology to a wide consumer base but, eventually, the goal should be to move away from the silos that society has built.*
- *Generally, recommends people to just try things out.*

Conclusion

Summary: Review of the points discussed.
Further Steps: Would you like to receive the final paper? **Yes.**

Thank you!

Appendix D Interview Transcript Stephan Rind (Bahnhofstrasse 52)

E. Schmid et al., *Tokenization in Real Estate*, SpringerBriefs in Finance,
https://doi.org/10.1007/978-3-031-55810-8

Interview Guide – Master Thesis

Interviewer: Elena Schmid...

Interviewee, Company: Stephan Rind, BrickMark...

Date, Location: 10.05.2022, Zollikon...

Introduction

Research Aim: Establish an overview of tokenization in real estate (technical, legal & current market situation). Form recommendations for market participants to broaden the application of tokenization in real estate (in Switzerland), based on secondary research and case studies.
Structure of Interview: Semi-structured interview with a guide for orientation. All information will be solely used for the purpose of this master thesis. The interview will last approximately 1 hour.

Interview

1. Background

Tell me about your background, what inspired/motivated you to work with the tokenization of real estate?

- *Many of their acquaintances were talking about blockchain, crypto and tokens in 2017. The world was changing and people started to invest. After spending some time reading up on the topic, it clicked. That was right before the crypto winter when a Bitcoin was worth around $13,000 and the general market capitalization of cryptos was at around $500 billion! Questions on how and why started to form.*
- *This was followed by a fascination for the technology, its decentralized manner, the consensus mechanism and trustless environment.*
- *The benefits of the technology was apparent as well as all potential further applications; let's take a traditional asset like real estate and put it on a blockchain. Through fractionalization everyday people can have access to the asset class – it would remove many of the hurdles which currently have to be overcome to invest in real estate.*
- *Then there is the cost aspect, 10-13% of sales proceeds are usually going to intermediaries which help to make a transaction happen. These costs could largely by reduced by using blockchain and tokens.*
- *Rind then decided to found BrickMark in 2017.*

2. Company-specific

Tell me about your company. What is your purpose/are your main goals? Why have you chosen to move from traditional real estate (investment) to blockchain?

- *"Das Ziel war eine Digitale Immobilien AG zu werden."*
- *However, BrickMark was still a bit early. As an example: Preos (German Immobiliengesellschaft) tokenized shares and Swiss Life is now a shareholder. However, for them such an investment is not equal to an investment in let's say a traditional real estate fund. It's still seen as a gamble from the perspective of institutional investors. Investors interested in digital assets are often looking high short- or medium-term returns as opposed to long-term steady returns.*
- *To introduce the technology and the concept of tokenization to the industry the first step is to set up a market for it. Here, the platform BrickGate comes into play. Most of the platform was already created for the purpose of BrickMark. Together with DSENT (technical provider) BrickGate was launched. The purpose of BrickGate is to become the biggest marketplace for real estate-backed tokens in Europe, sort of an Amazon for real estate.*

- *To reach that aim, BrickGate works with e.g., developers. Developers are having a hard time financing their projects ever since the financial crisis. Through BrickGate they can issue a token and finance their project with crowdfunding instead. BrickGate helps to navigate difficult decisions such as: should a fixed interest rate be chosen or a variable one? Should equity be tokenized instead of debt and token holders be payed dividends? etc. The platform is connected to a bank which can handle payments (InCore Bank), as most real estate (project) investors are still very traditional and might not have their own wallets or cryptocurrencies. In the future, when most investors are familiar with and use digital assets, the process could also be carried out without a bank.*
- *Generally, the idea is to "Markplätze über Grenzen hinweg zu schaffen." An agent in e.g., Beverly Hills has a client who wants to sell their luxury property. If the client agrees, the agent can, with the help of BrickGate, tokenize the asset as an NFT and put it on the BrickGate platform. Other agents around the world who are also connected to the platform have access to the NFT and can market it to their clients. If a transaction takes place the two agents share the fee. This concept increases the reach of the first agent and the offer of the second. It greatly expands the often very local market of real estate.*
- *The aim is to have a large, global network connecting a wide range of agents, investors and sellers. Tokenizing your asset instead of selling it in a traditional manner should simply be a choice by the seller.*
- *Additionally, once a real estate asset has been tokenized, the due diligence of said asset could be reduced by 50-80% should it be sold again a few years later as with the tokenization all related documents should have been verified and put on the blockchain as well.*
- *BrickGate gets a fee for structuring the process, placement, minting, and often also a success fee. They are open to receiving up to 50% of the fees in the form of tokens which were issued for the project. For each token/project there is a dashboard which shows who currently owns how many tokens. Only registered (KYC) investors can invest in the tokens and should they decide to transfer some of their tokens the new owner will also need to register and BrickMark will need to be notified about the exchange. Interest or dividends are only paid out to registered investors.*
- *Following the STO, BrickMark can also take care of lifecycle management e.g., paying out these dividends or interest. The tokens are then considered assets under management, and they receive a management fee. Meaning, the business model of BrickMark is not only project based but could also generate recurrent revenue streams.*
- *BrickMark currently has projects valued around $2 billion in their pipeline. However, some of the projects can be quite complex. For example, 'Innovative Living' in the US is a project on micro-apartments/student housing/co-living in close proximity to universities. The tokenization of the portfolio is difficult from a regulatory standpoint as there is not yet an elaborate framework in place. Communication with the SEC is therefore necessary. The project will most likely be treated similarly to an IPO. As a result, the pipeline which is currently projected could be delayed. Overall, the more interesting the projects and digital assets which can be launched are, the larger the interest (from potential investors) will be.*
- *Apart from BrickGate, BrickMark will continue to invest in real estate but mostly in 'Spezialimmobilien' such as castles. The BrickMark Token (BMT) has not yet been listed as there is no regulated exchange for it.*

3. Case-specific

3.1 Tell me about the tokenized asset(s), what have you achieved so far and how?
- *B52*

3.2 What elements were most important to successfully carry out the tokenization of an asset?
- *Convincing the seller to accept tokens as payment. RFR Holding, the previous owner of Bahnhofstrasse 52, is led by two private individuals – Germans, who moved to New York in the 90s and were able to buy and re-finance skyscrapers. They are interested in pushing the development of tokenization and therefore accepted 20% of the payment with BMTs, even*

though there is no guarantee that the token will be listed or is/will be worth anything. The 20% can be considered a 'vendor loan' or "Schuldschein".

- *Being able to carry out a transaction with a global institutional investor was difficult but very important as it sends a strong message.*

3.3 What were the biggest challenges you encountered?

- *The second biggest challenge was the regulatory part. The DLT act was not yet in place (2019/20) and even the big law firms were not sure what the criteria by FINMA would be, how a prospectus should be written, how the transaction should be structured etc. As a result, legal advice came at large costs. Also, when contacting FINMA to get feedback on certain issues, it could take 6-8 months for them to respond. The concepts were new and there were few regulators who had the necessary background to adequately judge them. If you don't know the risks of an investment it is difficult to set up a framework for it.*

3.4 What are your lessons learnt/what will you do differently with the next asset?

- *Since the tokenization of B52 the token industry in Switzerland has evolved. Now, there are certain product structures and frameworks for which regulations are clear. If you follow them, you can with be quite certain that your project can be carried out successfully. With B52, while everything was very new and interesting, it was also difficult and tiresome. Now, a client can approach BrickMark and they can give an overview of what the tokenization process will look like, a cost estimate and timeline.*
- *Also, in jurisdictions such as Switzerland, Germany or Luxembourg the general climate around tokenization and digital assets has developed positively. While a couple of years ago there was still a lot of uncertainty around blockchain and digital assets. Now, corporations such as JP Morgan and Goldman Sachs are working in the field and show that blockchain technology and tokens are innovations which can benefit all market players by saving costs, increasing efficiency and maybe even creating more intelligent products and offering new alternative investment opportunities.*
- *One of the main tasks right now is/should be education. People are starting to get interested in the topic. If you can explain the concepts well, people will start to understand all the possibilities and benefits which blockchain, digital assets and tokens hold. The more people who are convinced the more potential investors BrickGate will have at a later stage.*

3.5 What was the interest of your investors and how was the perception? Is there a demand for fractionalized and tokenized assets?

- *In the past 9-12 months, BrickMark/BrickGate has received more inquiries than they are able to work through.*
- *It is more difficult on the investor side; they will often say that they could just as well invest in a real estate fund. Creating an incentive for private investors to invest in real estate-backed tokens is difficult. However, 93% of the global real estate market is not (yet) publicly available. Also, when investing in a fund you can't specifically choose which asset to invest in.*

4. Personal Opinions & Recommendations

4.1 In your opinion, what are the current best practices for tokenizing real estate in the Swiss market?

- *Now, there are good guidelines/specifications by SDX on what a digital asset can look like. One of the main advantages of real estate tokens over traditional real estate is their tradability. Hence, why trading/exchange platforms for digital assets are so important.*
- *In terms of best practices, tokenizing a bond is the easiest way to go.*

4.2 What are your (specific) recommendations to the various market participants (investors, owners, legislators) going forward for successfully broadening the application of tokenization in the Swiss real estate market? OR What do the various market participants need to do, to take advantage of Switzerland being amongst the first movers?

- *Companies within the real estate industry should start building knowledge around the topic. Ideally, they have a designated person within their team focused on digitalization and blockchain. That person can then educate the rest of the team and clients can be introduced to the topic as well.*
- *As an example, Generali (who owns $40 billion in real estate asset) recently employed a Chief Digital Officer who is now analyzing the different branches of the company, establishing where efficiencies could be achieved through digitalization and how new products could be offered by implementing blockchain and tokens.*

4.3 What is your opinion on the future development of tokenization in real estate in Switzerland?

- *Many experts/players in the real estate markets have written reports on the topic of blockchain and tokenization and many have given projections on what development could look like in the future. While the timeline can differ from one report to another, all reports agree that there will be significant development at an increasingly higher rate. There will be a huge increase in digital assets, illiquid assets will be tokenized and a functioning secondary market available. The question is how quickly it will happen and not if it will happen. The timeline will largely depend on how quickly the different countries can outline a regulatory framework.*
- *As a comparison: Citibank in 1998 asked their clients whether they could see themselves accessing their bank accounts via internet or whether they could see themselves conducting payments via the internet. Over 95% answered no. They were worried about security. The aim is to have a similar story for tokenized real estate. People should be able to easily invest via their phones and not even worry about what technology is enabling the transactions.*
- *BrickMark want to be one of the biggest and well-known platforms for digital real estate and for offering such investment opportunities.*

4.4 What is your opinion on trends and the future development of tokenization in real estate on a global level? What are the main "competing" countries?

- *NFT sales of real estate are already happening in the US. While their regulations are not as elaborate yet, market players are very creative and 'just do stuff'. Meanwhile, Rind does not really consider Liechtenstein a competitive country, however, Germany is developing strongly. Dubai has a new DLT Act which should be coming into force this year. Singapore is also far ahead, and Australia will have an exchange similar to SDX. Japan is currently setting up a decentralized exchange for digital assets.*

5. Final Question

Do you have a final comment/advisement to add?

Conclusion

Summary: Review of the points discussed.
Further Steps: Would you like to receive the final paper? **Yes.**

Thank you!

Appendix E Interview Transcript Dadvan Yousuf (Crowdlitoken Portfolio)

E. Schmid et al., *Tokenization in Real Estate*, SpringerBriefs in Finance,
https://doi.org/10.1007/978-3-031-55810-8

Interview Guide – Master Thesis
Tokenization in Real Estate

HSLU Hochschule Luzern

Interview Guide – Master Thesis

Interviewer: Elena Schmid...

Interviewee, Company: Dadvan Yousuf, Crowdlitoken...

Date, Location: 06.04.2022, Bern (phone call)...

Introduction

Research Aim: Establish an overview of tokenization in real estate (technical, legal & current market situation). Form recommendations for market participants to broaden the application of tokenization in real estate (in Switzerland), based on secondary research and case studies.
Structure of Interview: Semi-structured interview with a guide for orientation. All information will be solely used for the purpose of this master thesis. The interview will last approximately 1 hour.

Interview

1. Background

Tell me about your background, what inspired/motivated you to work with the tokenization of real estate?

2. Company-specific

Tell me about your company. What is your purpose/are your main goals? Why have you chosen to move from traditional real estate (investment) to blockchain?

- *It is to democratize real estate investments. Everyone should be able to take part in the real estate investment market, even with just a CHF 100.*
- *Currently the focus is just on demand/supply, their offer satisfies a demand of the market, and Crowdlitoken has found a way to tokenize assets with an intermediate ownership form.*
- *However, Yousuf wants to further develop the company in the future but was vague around the exact strategy. It could go into the direction of offering individuals a platform to tokenize their private homes or raise capital to finance their homes.*

3. Case-specific

3.1 Tell me about the tokenized asset(s), what have you achieved so far and how?

- *Two tokenized assets, only available on the Crowdlitoken platform.*
- *They currently use an intermediate ownership form.*
- *Liquidity is still a problem, their platform can currently only trade tokens if there is both supply and demand – a secondary market exchange is still missing, worldwide. That is currently one of the challenges the industry is facing for the broad application of tokenization.*

3.2 What elements were most important to successfully carry out the tokenization of an asset?

3.3 What were the biggest challenges you encountered?

3.4 What are your lessons learnt/what will you do differently with the next asset?

3.5 What was the interest of your investors and how was the perception? Is there a demand for fractionalized and tokenized assets?

1

4. Personal Opinions & Recommendations

4.1 In your opinion, what are the current best practices for tokenizing real estate in the Swiss market?

4.2 What are your (specific) recommendations to the various market participants (investors, owners, legislators) going forward for successfully broadening the application of tokenization in the Swiss real estate market? OR What do the various market participants need to do, to take advantage of Switzerland being amongst the first movers?

- *Yousuf does not see laws or regulations as the crucial elements which will further or hinder the development of tokenization in real estate BUT*
- *Inform the masses! Currently the largest problem is that people do not understand what a token is, they don't understand crypto or blockchain and will therefore also not trust and/or be interested in investing through/in this new technology. There is a huge education gap, and a huge cap in know-how.*
- *Yousuf deems cryptos to be highly untransparent and it's a young technology. However, more and more people are becoming interested in it. In comparison, it should be easier to explain the concept of a security token as it is a digital representation of an actual underlying asset.*
- *Yousuf is also the CEO of Dohrnii, a platform which they describe works similar to duolingo. The aim is to educate and empower people on everything 'cypto & investing'.*

4.3 What is your opinion on the future development of tokenization in real estate in Switzerland?

- *As mentioned, laws and regulations won't make the difference, but education will.*
- *The Swiss real estate market is highly interesting, and especially also highly attractive to international investors – Swiss real estate is somewhat of a safe haven. However, with Lex Koller/Lex Friedrich international investors are not allowed to invest in residential buildings in Switzerland apart from personal use. With the tokenization of properties, this could be bypassed, or, could currently be bypassed as long as the laws don't change. So, an international investor could hold e.g., 30% of the tokens of a Swiss residential property and directly profit from rental income and appreciation of the property.*
- *Yousuf understands that some support the Lex Koller/Lex Friedrich laws as it protects the Swiss residential real estate market from price increases as a result of high international demand but believes that everyone should be allowed to invest in everything, everywhere and that the law shouldn't discriminate against foreigners in their investment decisions.*

4.4 What is your opinion on trends and the future development of tokenization in real estate on a global level? What are the main "competing" countries?

- *Tokens will be used for a healthy diversification of portfolios on a global level – this will include NFTs, and various security tokens including real estate tokens.*
- *On a practical level, it won't be the real estate asset itself which is tokenized but the economic rights related to the ownership of the asset. For example: should you want to buy a house, you will most likely need a mortgage. The bank, in turn, will want security and a down payment before granting you the mortgage. In Switzerland, the down payment is often 20% or higher, making it impossible for many to afford it. Tokens offer an alternative to raising capital. You can tokenize the economic rights to the property you are buying or the debt you require and then issue tokens for the masses to buy and finance your home – it is a new way of crowdfunding. On which platform this could happen is still unclear.*
- *This example also works the other way around. Imagine you already own a home but are in need of capital, you could now tokenize the economic rights to parts of your home and sell them to interested investors to raise capital for a different endeavor.*

Interview Guide – Master Thesis
Tokenization in Real Estate

HSLU Hochschule Luzern

5. Final Question

Do you have a final comment/advisement to add?

- *Tokenization in real estate will be the future. Currently it is still a bit too early, but Yousuf sees a broader application within the next 5 years.*

Conclusion

Summary: Review of the points discussed.
Further Steps: Would you like to receive the final paper? **No.**

Thank you!

Appendix F Interview Transcript Simon Büchi (Crowdlitoken Portfolio)

E. Schmid et al., *Tokenization in Real Estate*, SpringerBriefs in Finance, https://doi.org/10.1007/978-3-031-55810-8

Interview Guide – Master Thesis

Interviewer: Elena Schmid...

Interviewee, Company: Simon Büchi, Crowdlitoken..

Date, Location: 08.04.2022, Luzern (phone call)...

Introduction

Research Aim: Establish an overview of tokenization in real estate (technical, legal & current market situation). Form recommendations for market participants to broaden the application of tokenization in real estate (in Switzerland), based on secondary research and case studies.
Structure of Interview: Semi-structured interview with a guide for orientation. All information will be solely used for the purpose of this master thesis. The interview will last approximately 1 hour.

Interview

1. Background

Tell me about your background, what inspired/motivated you to work with the tokenization of real estate?

2. Company-specific

Tell me about your company. What is your purpose/are your main goals? Why have you chosen to move from traditional real estate (investment) to blockchain?

- *Their main goal is to offer investment possibilities even with just a small budget, starting at CHF 100.*
- *Blockchain was/is the right platform for this endeavor. However, it did not necessarily have to work on a blockchain, but it works well, especially due to it being a very (data) secure platform.*
- *The goal is to tokenize and offer as many properties on the platform as possible, and, therefore, offer as many investment opportunities as possible.*
- *With the change in CEO to Dadvan Yousuf there is a new financing strategy in the works. Currently, Crowdlitoken is buying real estate with its own equity and by getting a mortgage – so traditional financing of real estate. However, with this strategy you also need high amounts of equity. The new strategy aims to reserve the property from the seller for around 1-2 months. Within this timeframe the goal is then to convince as many investors as possible of the investment opportunity and have them buy tokens and place them on the property. If enough tokens are placed the property can be bought by Crowdlitoken (it will still be legally owned by the company) and put on the platform. So, a sort of crowdfunding strategy. Still, naturally, around 50% of financing will come from a mortgage.*
- *At first, probably both strategies are going to be applied side-by-side. Should the crowdfunding strategy work well, they might switch to it entirely.*

3. Case-specific

3.1 Tell me about the tokenized asset(s), what have you achieved so far and how?

3.2 What elements were most important to successfully carry out the tokenization of an asset?

- *You still need to find good business opportunities, choose good properties, do your valuations well, etc. So, business as usual.*
- *Then, as opposed to selling through an intermediary or a bank, you sell directly, upfront to the investors.*

- *The Crowdlitoken portfolio currently has two properties. They are, on paper, not very exciting. They are two commercial properties. However, they achieve good returns and a good yield (paid out on a monthly basis to the investors).*
- *On a technical level the platform needs to work seamlessly as well, payments and transactions must go through. There was some trial and error to make it work.*
- *Also, the tokenization itself is not rocket science anymore. However, it still needs to be done and it needs to be done well, which also took some time.*

3.3 What were the biggest challenges you encountered?

- *Compliance and legal aspects: Crowdlitoken worked hard and long and invested a lot of money to create their prospectus, get the right licenses and make sure the entire business strategy was legal and approved by FINMA. This was important to make sure the business strategy would be attractive to investors. The result is a business strategy and investment offer which is unique in Switzerland.*
- *Getting new money is also big challenge. To continuously convince new investors of the concept is difficult and can take time. Marketing is necessary.*

3.4 What are your lessons learnt/what will you do differently with the next asset?

- *There is a pipeline but currently the focus lies on on-boarding new investors and new money. For the two already tokenized properties there is still capacity for investors to invest/place their tokens. Buying a third property is unnecessary at this point in time.*
- *However, tokenizing and putting up a third property on the Crowdlitoken platform would not be a problem and could be done within days.*

3.5 What was the interest of your investors and how was the perception? Is there a demand for fractionalized and tokenized assets?

- *Generally, yes, but in their opinion investors aren't necessarily looking for tokens to invest in but for secure investments overall. Also, there is demand for smaller investments (of course Crowdlitoken always tries to upsell and have investors place a higher amount or have them invest on a repeating basis, but even a CHF 100 investment is already profitable for Crowdlitoken).*
- *Also, people are increasingly more interested in investing in real estate.*
- *So, the interest is clearly there but it is not a 'Selbstläufer'. You need to first explain the business model to the potential investors. Crowdlitoken is not and does not want to be a hip, fancy crypto/blockchain firm but a modern and secure investment platform – comparable to the various '3. Säule' apps, offering a stable investment and stable yield.*

4. Personal Opinions & Recommendations

4.1 In your opinion, what are the current best practices for tokenizing real estate in the Swiss market?

- *Tokenization is still a young and small business concept. However, a lot is being tokenized right now – art, currencies (in stablecoin) and other financial products.*
- *One can't say that Crowdlitoken has found THE best way to tokenize a real estate asset, but probably no one has. There is no current dominant player in the real estate token market, everyone is doing it on a trial-and-error basis.*
- *However, Crowdlitoken is convinced of the future role of tokenization in general, especially in the real estate market. Tokens hold true benefits/real advantages like increased liquidity, easier access to the real estate market and lower threshold/barrier to the market. For tokenization to work there need to be such benefits.*

4.2 What are your (specific) recommendations to the various market participants (investors, owners, legislators) going forward for successfully broadening the application of tokenization in the Swiss real estate market? OR What do the various market participants need to do, to take advantage of Switzerland being amongst the first movers?

4.3 What is your opinion on the future development of tokenization in real estate in Switzerland?

4.4 What is your opinion on trends and the future development of tokenization in real estate on a global level? What are the main "competing" countries?

5. Final Question
Do you have a final comment/advisement to add?

Conclusion

Summary: Review of the points discussed.
Further Steps: Would you like to receive the final paper? **Yes.**

Thank you!

References

Allison, I. (2021, June 7). Remember JPM Coin? Next step is programmable money, Bank Exec Says. *Coin Desk*. https://www.coindesk.com/business/2021/06/07/remember-jpm-coin-next-step-is-programmable-money-bank-exec-says/

Ammous, S. (2016). Can cryptocurrencies fulfil the functions of money? *The Quarterly Review of Economics and Finance, 70*, 38–51. https://doi.org/10.1016/j.qref.2018.05.010

Arslanian, H., Donovan, R., Blumenfeld, M., & Zamore, A. (2021). El Salvador's law: a meaningful test for Bitcoin. *PwC*. https://www.pwc.com/gx/en/financial-services/pdf/el-salvadors-law-a-meaningful-test-for-bitcoin.pdf

Baum, A. (2020). Tokenisation - the future of real estate investment? *The Journal of Portfolio Management Real Estate, 47*(10), 41–61. https://doi.org/10.3905/jpm.2021.1.260

Becker, A., & Blassl, J. (2021, September 22). Was es beim Launch des Kryptowertpapierregisters zu beachten gilt. *EY*. https://www.ey.com/de_de/financial-services/dies-gilt-es-beim-kryptowertpapierregister-zu-beachten

Bell, E., Bryman, A., & Harley, B. (2019). *Business research methods* (5th ed.). Oxford University Press.

Berentsen, A., & Markheim, M. (2020). Real estate meets blockchain opportunities and challenges of tokenization of illiquid Assets. *Munich Personal RePEc Archive,* (99399). https://mpra.ub.uni-muenchen.de/102276/1/

Bitcoin Suisse. (2019, October 24). *The Opportunities of Liechtenstein's New Blockchain Act*. https://www.bitcoinsuisse.com/news/the-opportunities-of-liechtensteins-new-blockchain-act

blockimmo. (2018, November 12). *Facilitating an accessible & streamlined real estate market*. https://blockimmo.ch/about

blockimmo. (2019, June 8). *First Rent Payout for Tokenholders of "HelloWorld"*. Medium. https://medium.com/blockimmo/first-rent-payout-for-tokenholders-of-helloworld-e0f0fcbfbf55

blockimmo. (n.d.). *About*. Retrieved March 20, 2022, from https://blockimmo.ch/about

Bortz, J., & Döring, N. (2009). *Forschungsmethoden und Evaluation* (4th ed.). Springer.

BrickMark. (n.d.). *BrickMark*. Retrieved March 22, 2022, from https://brickmark.net

BrickMark, A. G. (2020, January 15). *BrickMark signs purchase agreement for the largest ever real estate transaction paid in tokens of a total volume of over CHF 130 million*. Medium. https://medium.com/brickmark-ag/brickmark-signs-purchase-agreement-for-the-largest-ever-real-estate-transaction-paid-in-tokens-of-13a6195cb303

Bricktrade. (n.d.). *About Us*. Retrieved May 13, 2022 from https://bricktrade.co.uk/aboutus

Bundesgesetz betreffend die Ergänzung des Schweizerischen Zivilgesetzbuches. (1911). (Fünfter Teil: Obligationenrecht) [OR], AS 27 317, Art. 216.

E. Schmid et al., *Tokenization in Real Estate*, SpringerBriefs in Finance,
https://doi.org/10.1007/978-3-031-55810-8

Bundesministerium für Finanzen. (n.d.). *Blockchain-Strategie der Bundesregierung*. Retrieved May 13, 2022, from https://www.blockchain-strategie.de/BC/Navigation/DE/Home/home.html

Business Insider India. (2022, March 11). *Dubai adopts crypto law as it looks to become a hub for web 3.0*. https://www.businessinsider.in/cryptocurrency/news/dubai-adopts-crypto-law-as-it-looks-to-become-a-hub-for-web-3-0/articleshow/90146919.cms

cadastre.ch (a). *Objectives & organisation*. Retrieved March 8, 2022, from https://www.cadastre.ch/en/gb/objective.html

cadastre.ch (b). *Cooperation between federal government, cantons & the private sector*. Retrieved March 8, 2022, from https://www.cadastre.ch/en/av/objective.html

Cashlink. (n.d.). *Shaping the capital markets of tomorrow*. Retrieved May 13, 2022, from https://cashlink.de

Castor, A. (2022, March 4). Why Ethereum is switching to proof of stake and how it will work. *MIT Technology Review*. https://www.technologyreview.com/2022/03/04/1046636/ethereum-blockchain-proof-of-stake/

Ceccon, M. (2021, October 28). What happens when buildings own and manage themselves? *EY*. https://www.ey.com/en_ch/strategy/what-happens-when-buildings-own-and-manage-themselves

Chainalysis. (2022, January 6). *Crypto Crime Trends for 2022: Illicit Transaction Activity Reaches All-Time High in Value, All-Time Low in Share of All Cryptocurrency Activity*. https://blog.chainalysis.com/reports/2022-crypto-crime-report-introduction/

Chang, S. E., & Chen, Y. (2020). When blockchain meets supply chain: A systematic literature review on current development and potential applications. *IEEE Access, 8*, 62478–62494. https://doi.org/10.1109/ACCESS.2020.2983601

Comply Advantage. (n.d.). *Cryptocurrency in Australia: Regulations & laws*. Retrieved May 13, 2022, from https://complyadvantage.com/insights/crypto-regulations/cryptocurrency-regulations-australia/

Crowdlitoken. (2019, May 15). *Real estate strategy*. https://crowdlitoken.com/wp-content/uploads/doc/immostgy/real_estate_strategy_en.pdf

Crowdlitoken. (2020, April 23). *CHF 16 million successfully invested thanks to digital real estate investment*. https://crowdlitoken.com/news/chf-16-million-successfully-invested-thanks-to-digital-real-estate-investment/?lang=en

Crowdlitoken. (2020b, December 9). *CROWDLITOKEN becomes officially tradable - Digital assets become more and more tangible*. https://crowdlitoken.com/news/crowdlitoken-becomes-officially-tradable-digital-assets-become-more-and-more-tangible/?lang=en

Crowdlitoken. (2021, January 14). *CROWDLITOKEN AG is registered by the FMA*. https://crowdlitoken.com/news/crowdlitoken-ag-receives-the-new-blockchain-license-in-liechtenstein/?lang=en

Crowdlitoken (a). *About us*. Retrieved March 22, 2022, from https://crowdlitoken.com/about-us/?lang=en.

Crowdlitoken (b). *How it works*. Retrieved March 22, 2022, from https://crowdlitoken.com/how-it-works/?lang=en.

Crowdlitoken (c). *Real estate*. Retrieved March 23, 2022, from https://crowdlitoken.com/real-estate/?lang=en.

CSSF. (2022, January 24). *The CSSF published a white paper on DLT and blockchain*. https://www.cssf.lu/en/2022/01/the-cssf-published-a-white-paper-on-dlt-and-blockchain/

de la Rubia, C., Sandner, P., & Gross, J. (2021). *Studie zur Tokenisierung von Immobilien*. https://www.hcob-bank.de/media/pdf_3/presse/publikationen/studien/2021_2/studie_tokenisierung_immobilien_2021.pdf

Deloitte. (2021). Real estate STO whitepaper. https://www2.deloitte.com/content/dam/Deloitte/cn/Documents/real-estate/deloitte-cn-real-estate-sto-whitepaper-1st-paper-report-en-210819.pdf

Deloitte. (2022, March 17). *Digital Finance: European Parliament adopts MiCA Regulation, paving the way for an innovation-friendly crypto regulation*. https://www2.deloitte.com/lu/en/

pages/financial-services/articles/digital-finance-european-parliament-adopts-mica-regulation-innovation-friendly-crypto-regulation.html

Deloitte. (n.d.). *Blockchain services and solutions*. Retrieved May 14, 2022, from https://www2.deloitte.com/kz/en/pages/strategy-operations/solutions/blockchain-services-and-solutions.html

Dewey, J. (2022, May 13). Blockchain & Cryptocurrency Laws and Regulations 2022 - USA. *Global Legal Insights*. https://www.globallegalinsights.com/practice-areas/blockchain-laws-and-regulations/usa

Dietrich, A. (2022, April 4). Wird die Zukunft von Bankdienstleistungen auf dem Metaverse beruhen? *Hochschule Luzern*. https://blog.hslu.ch/retailbanking/2022/04/04/wird-die-zukunft-von-bankdienstleistungen-auf-dem-metaverse-beruhen/

Dietz, M. (2019, January 30). Introducing blockimmo's platform smart contracts v2. *Medium*. https://medium.com/blockimmo/introducing-blockimmos-platform-smart-contracts-v2-d40657aff255

Digibrixx. (n.d.). *DIGIBRIXX the new metric to invest in real estate programmes*. Retrieved May 13, 2022, from https://www.digibrixx.eu/#

DigiShares. (2022). *Tokenization of Real Estate - Best Practices*. https://digishares.io/pdf

Don, B. (2021, April 14). *Token Factory: Real Estate and Blockchain* [PowerPoint slides]. Rotkreuz, Switzerland.

Eidgenössische Steuerverwaltung. (n.d.). *Kryptowährungen - Besteuerung*. Retrieved May 6, 2022, from https://www.estv.admin.ch/estv/de/home/direkte-bundessteuer/fachinformationen-dbst/kryptowaehrungen.html

European Commission. (2020, September 24). *Digital finance package*. https://ec.europa.eu/info/publications/200924-digital-finance-proposals_en

EY (n.d.). *Blockchain platforms*. Retrieved May 14, 2022, from https://www.ey.com/en_ch/blockchain/blockchain-platforms

Finexity. (n.d.). *Invest in alternative assets. Fully digital and flexible*. Retrieved May 13, 2022, from https://finexity.com

FINMA. (n.d.). *Licensing as a DLT trading facility*. Retrieved March 30, 2022, from https://www.finma.ch/en/authorisation/fintech/dlt-handelssystem/

Flick, U. (2010). *Qualitative Sozialforschung* (3rd ed.). Rowohlt.

Fonnesbæk Lodahl, J. (2021). Real Estate Tokenization - An Industry Report. *DigiShares*. https://digishares.io/pdf

Franklin, J. (2021, December 20). JPMorgan develops blockchain system for Siemens' payments. *Financial Times*. https://www.ft.com/content/e14582fc-a154-4c96-9d65-9bc86c89a7a3

Fraxtor. (n.d.). *Access Real Estate Opportunities with Ease*. Retrieved May 13, 2022, from https://www.fraxtor.com/about/

Fries, T. (2021, May 24). $134M Zurich Real Estate Sold with 20% of Price Paid with Security Tokens. *The Tokenist*. https://tokenist.com/134m-zurich-real-estate-sold-with-20-of-price-paid-with-security-tokens/

Galaxy Digital. (2022, March 21). *Galaxy Digital Facilitates Goldman Sachs's First OTC Crypto Options Trade*. https://investor.galaxydigital.io/news/news-details/2022/Galaxy-Digital-Facilitates-Goldman-Sachss-First-OTC-Crypto-Options-Trade/default.aspx

Generali Investments. (2022, April 13). *Generali Investments and Generali IARD carry-out first market transaction based on blockchain infrastructure*. https://www.generali-investments.com/it/en/institutional/article/generali-investments-and-generali-iard-carry-out-first-market-transaction-based-on-blockchain-infrastructure

Goldman Sachs. (2021, June 10). *Digitizing Bonds on the Blockchain*. https://www.goldmansachs.com/insights/pages/from_briefings_10-june-2021.html

Graglia, J., & Mellon, C. (2018). Blockchain and property in 2018: At the end of the beginning. *Innovations: Technology, Governance, Globalization, 12*(1–2), 90–116. https://doi.org/10.1162/inov_a_00270

Harbor. (n.d.). *Transforming the alternative investment experience*. Retrieved May 13, 2022, from https://harbor.com

Hässig, L. (2022, May 20). Aufstieg und Fall eines Krypto-Prinzen. *Inside Paradeplatz*. https://insideparadeplatz.ch/2022/05/20/aufstieg-und-fall-eines-krypto-prinzen/

HM Treasury. (2022, April 4). *Government sets out plan to make UK a global cryptoasset technology hub*. https://www.gov.uk/government/news/government-sets-out-plan-to-make-uk-a-global-cryptoasset-technology-hub

Hopf-Sulc, A. (2022, April 4). Er verspricht Reichtum auf Instagram - nun hat er die Finma am Hals. *Tagesanzeiger*. https://www.tagesanzeiger.ch/er-verspricht-reichtum-auf-instagram-nun-hat-er-die-finma-am-hals-239529921324

Hoxha, V., & Sadiku, S. (2019). Study of factors influencing the decision to adopt the blockchain technology in real estate transactions in Kosovo. *Property Management, 37*(5), 684–700. https://doi.org/10.1108/PM-01-2019-0002

Jacoby, S. (2021, January 28). Luxembourg law recognises the use of DLT for the issuance of dematerialised securities. *Clifford Chance*. https://www.cliffordchance.com/briefings/2021/01/luxembourg-law-recognises-the-use-of-dlt-for-the-issuance-of-dem.html

Jyotsna, Y., & Gampala, K. (2020). Blockchain for Real Estate. https://www.researchgate.net/profile/Jyotsna-Yarlagadda-2/publication/347442436_Blockchain_for_Real_Estate/links/5fdc20f492851c13fe959c9d/Blo ckchain-for-Real-Estate.pdf

Konashevych, O. (2020). General concept of real estate tokenization on blockchain. *European Property Law Journal, 9*(1), 21–65. https://doi.org/10.1515/eplj-2020-0003

LABS. (n.d.). *Transforming Real Estate into Digital Shares*. Retrieved May 13, 2022, from https://cf.labsgroup.io

Lai, A., Pang, P., Lee, E., Murphy, J., Wu, J., Pecenicic, E., & Blanchoz, S. (2020). Tokenisation of Alternative Investments. *CAIA Association*. https://caia.org/sites/default/files/2021-02/CAIA_Tokenisation_of_Alternatives.pdf

Lapin, N. (2021, December 23). Explaining Crypto's 9olatility. *Forbes*. https://www.forbes.com/sites/nicolelapin/2021/12/23/explaining-cryptos-volatility/?sh=1bcef69b7b54

Laurent, P., Chollet, T., Burke, M., & Seers, T. (2018). The tokenization of assets is disrupting the financial industry. Are you ready? *Deloitte*. https://www2.deloitte.com/content/dam/Deloitte/cz/Documents/financial-services/Deloitte_Inside_19_CIO_Edition_Nov_2018.pdf

Ledger Insights. (2021, October 7). *MUFG, SBI share roadmap for Japanese security tokens*. https://www.ledgerinsights.com/mufg-sbi-share-roadmap-for-japanese-security-token-platform/

Lee, P. (2022, April 19). EU crypto regulation update (April 2022): EU Bitcoin ban shelved - and MiCA moves forward. *Lexology*. https://www.lexology.com/library/detail.aspx?g=3cb536e3-64d7-46cb-8c2e-3d3f9df6e05d

Liu, N., Duncan, R., & Chapman, A. (2020). A critical review of distributed ledger technology and its applications in real estate. *Royal Institution of Chartered Surveyors (RICS)*. https://www.rics.org/globalassets/rics-website/media/knowledge/research/research-reports/rics0077-001-distributed-ledger-technology-review-report%2D%2Dfinal.pdf

Loh, D. (2022, April 5). Singapore's crypto players face added scrutiny under new law. *NIKKEI Asia*. https://asia.nikkei.com/Spotlight/Cryptocurrencies/Singapore-s-crypto-players-face-added-scrutiny-under-new-law

Luchsinger, C. (2021, November 30). *Tokenization of Real Estate: The Swiss Legal Perspective*. [PowerPoint slides]. Zug, Switzerland.

Luchsinger, C. (2022, January 18). Tokenisierung von Grundstücken in der Schweiz - eine Bestandesaufnahme. *MLL News*. https://www.mll-news.com/tokenisierung-von-grundstuecken-in-der-schweiz-eine-bestandesaufnahme/

Maull, R., Godsiff, P., Mulligan, C., Brown, A., & Kewell, B. (2017). Distributed ledger technology: Applications and implications. *Strategic Change, 26*(5), 481–489. https://doi.org/10.1002/jsc.2148

moneycab. (2019, March 1). *«Hello World» aus dem Crypto Valley: erste Immobilien-Transaktion auf Blockchain.* https://www.moneycab.com/it/digitalisierung/hello-world-aus-dem-crypto-valley-erste-immobilien-transaktion-auf-blockchain/

Monrat, A., Schelén, O., & Andersson, K. (2019). A survey of blockchain from the perspectives of applications, challenges, and opportunities. *IEEE, 7*, 117134–117151. https://doi.org/10.1109/ACCESS.2019.2936094

Morgan, J. P. (n.d.). *Blockchain Center of Excellence*. Retrieved May 14, 2022, from https://www.jpmorgan.com/insights/technology/blockchain

MountX. (n.d.). *Investment Projects*. Retrieved May 13, 2022, from https://mountx.io/en/inversores-inversionistas-mountx/

Nakamoto, S. (2008, October 31). Bitcoin: A peer-to-peer electronic cash system. *Decentralized Business Review*, 21260. https://www.debr.io/articles

Natarajan, H., Krause, S., & Gradstein, H. (2017). Distributed Ledger Technology (DLT) and Blockchain. *World Bank Group*. https://openknowledge.worldbank.org/handle/10986/29053.

Nijland, M., & Veuger, J. (2019). Influence of blockchain in the real estate sector: In which stage of the buying process of commercial real estate can blockchain provide added value for the stakeholders involved? *International Journal of Applied Science, 2*(2), 22–40. https://doi.org/10.30560/ijas.v2n2p22

Nofer, M., Gomber, P., Hinz, O., & Schiereck, D. (2017). Blockchain. *Business & Information. Systems Engineering, 59*(3), 183–187. https://doi.org/10.1007/s12599-017-0467-3

ODX Co. Ltd. (n.d.). *About*. Retrieved May 13, 2022, from https://www.odx.co.jp/en/corporate/about/

Oliveira, L., Zavolokina, L., Bauer, I., & Schwabe, G. (2018). To token or not to token: Tools for understanding blockchain tokens [Conference session]. International Conference of Information Systems, San Francisco, USA. https://doi.org/10.5167/uzh-157908

Oliver, J. (2022, May 15). Goldman Sachs and Barclays bank invest in Alan Howard's crypto platform. *Financial Times*. https://www.ft.com/content/2e44ca65-1085-4429-b82a-5a6912ec1e65

Oliver, J., & Stafford, P. (2022, April 28). Why the UK joined the race to woo the crypto industry. *Financial Times*. https://www.ft.com/content/65eb9636-d253-42af-8526-50d70c41a19b

Pang, P., Tang, H., Lam, J., Chan, J., Hobler, N., & Kan, K. (2020). Real Estate Tokenization. *Liquefy, Sidley, KPMG, Colliers International*. https://assets.kpmg/content/dam/kpmg/cn/pdf/en/2020/04/real-estate-tokenization.pdf

Pankratov, E., Grigoryev, V., & Pankratov, O. (2020). The blockchain technology in real estate sector: Experience and prospects. *IOP Conference Series: Materials Science and Engineering, 869*(6), 062010. https://doi.org/10.1088/1757-899X/869/6/062010

Pauli, S. (2022, May 5). Staatsanwaltschaft eröffnet Verfahren gegen «Krypto-King» Yousuf. *SRF*. https://www.srf.ch/news/wirtschaft/unter-geldwaescherei-verdacht-staatsanwaltschaft-eroeffnet-verfahren-gegen-krypto-king-yousuf

Pauli, S., & Jaquemart, C. (2022, February 17). Der Krypto-«Milliardär» und seine fragwürdigen Transaktionen. *SRF*. https://www.srf.ch/news/wirtschaft/krypto-king-dadvan-yousuf-der-krypto-milliardaer-und-seine-fragwuerdigen-transaktionen

Pereire, K., & YingXin, L. (n.d.). *Blockchain & Cryptocurrency Laws and Regulations 2022 - Singapore*. Retrieved May 13, 2022, from https://www.globallegalinsights.com/practice-areas/blockchain-laws-and-regulations/singapore

PwC. (2022a, March 30). Swiss DLT law: New regulations bring new opportunities. *PwC*. https://www.pwc.ch/en/insights/regulation/swiss-dlt-new-regulations.html

PwC. (2022b, January). PwC Annual Global Crypto Tax Report 2021. *PwC*. https://www.pwc.com/gx/en/insights/pwc-annual-global-crypto-tax-report-2021.pdf

Rauchs, M., Glidden, A., Gordon, B., Pieters, G., Recanatini, M., Rostand, F., & Zhang, B. (2018). *Distributed ledger technology system: A conceptual framework*. Center for Alternative Finance. https://doi.org/10.2139/ssrn.3230013

RealT. (n.d.). *Fractional and frictionless real estate investing*. Retrieved May 13, 2022, from https://realt.co

RedSwan C. R. E. (n.d.). *A Tokenized Commercial Real Estate Marketplace*. Retrieved May 13, 2022, from https://redswan.io

Rind, S. (2021a). *Immobilientoken - die Zukunf des Immobilieninvestments*. Ringier Axel Springer.

Rind, S. (2021b, November 30). BrickMark: Next level real estate investments [PowerPoint slides]. Zug, Switzerland.

Rind, S. (2022, May 03). BrickMark Group: Next level real estate investments [Conference session]. Fachkonferenz Real Estate Investment und Asset Management. Rotkreuz, Switzerland.

Risius, M., & Spohrer, K. (2017). A blockchain research framework: What we (don't) know, where we go from here, and how we will get there. *Business & Information Systems Engineering, 59*(6), 385–409. https://doi.org/10.1007/s12599-017-0506-0

Schweizerisches Zivilgesetzbuch [ZGB]. (1907). AS 24 233, Art. 656.

Schweizerisches Zivilgesetzbuch [ZGB]. (1907). AS 24 233, Art. 948.

Scott, J. (1990). *A matter of record: Documentary sources in social research*. Polity Press.

Shabbir, M. U. (2021). Blockchain in real estate sector: benefits and challenges. https://www.researchgate.net/publication/348501705_Blockchain_in_Real_Estate_Sector_Benefits_and_Challenges

Shahnaz, A., Qamar, U., & Khalid, A. (2019). Using blockchain for electronic health records. *IEEE Access, 7*, 147782–147795. https://doi.org/10.1109/ACCESS.2019.2946373

SIX. (2021, November 18). *SIX launches its SIX digital exchange by successfully issuing the World's first digital bond in a fully regulated environment*. https://www.six-group.com/en/newsroom/media-releases/2021/20211118-six-sdx-digital-bond.html

Smith, J., Vora, M., Benedetti, H., Yoshida, K., & Vogel, Z. (2019). Tokenized securities & commercial real estate. *MIT Digital Currency Initiative*. https://mitcre.mit.edu/wp-content/uploads/2019/11/Tokenized-Security-Commercial-Real-Estate2.pdf

Sonenreich, A. (2022, February 16). NFTs and the future of commercial real estate. *Forbes*. https://www.forbes.com/sites/forbesbusinesscouncil/2022/02/16/nfts-and-the-future-of-commercial-real-estate/?sh=15f2e6c59bac

Spett, S. (2020, January 16). Brickmark Makes Largest Real Estate Transaction with Tokens. *Switzerland Global Enterprise*. https://www.s-ge.com/en/article/news/20201-blockchain-brickmark

Stefano, R. (2021, August 4). Immobilienbesitz per Smartphone. *Neue Züricher Zeitung*. https://www.nzz.ch/themen-dossiers/zukunft-bauen/immobilienbesitz-per-smartphone-ld.1633330

Stefanoski, D., Sahin, O., Banusch, B., Fuchs, S., Andermatt, S., & Quertramp, A. (2020). Tokenization of Assets. *EY*. https://assets.ey.com/content/dam/ey-sites/ey-com/en_ch/topics/blockchain/ey-tokenization-of-assets-broschure-final.pdf

Sull, A., & Baum, A. (2019, March). The Future of Real Estate Transactions. *University of Oxford Research*. https://www.sbs.ox.ac.uk/sites/default/files/2019-03/FoRET-ReportSummary_0.pdf

Swan, M. (2015). *Blockchain: Blueprint for a new economy*. O'Reilly Media, Inc.

SwissRealCoin. (n.d.). *Switzerland's first real estate crypto token*. Retrieved May 11, 2022, from https://www.swissrealcoin.io/#what-is-src

swisstopo. (2017). *The Swiss Cadastral System: a basis for security and prosperity*. https://www.swisstopo.admin.ch/en/knowledge-facts/swiss-cadastral-surveying/cadastral-surveying.html

Sygnum. (n.d.). *About us*. Retrieved May 14, 2022, from https://www.sygnum.com/about-us/

Szabo, N. (1997). Formalizing and securing relationships on public networks. *First Monday, 2*(9). https://doi.org/10.5210/fm.v2i9.548

Szalay, E., & Stafford, P. (2021, December 13). HSBC and Wells Fargo to settle currency trades with blockchain. *Financial Times*. https://www.ft.com/content/1a4dcaf5-2b4b-4f0b-8c58-a8f-a173f24b3

The Federal Council. (2018, December 14). *Legal framework for distributed ledger technology and blockchain in Switzerland*. https://www.newsd.admin.ch/newsd/message/attachments/55153.pdf

The Federal Council. (2021, December 28). *Federal Council brings DLT Act fully into force and issues ordinance.* https://www.admin.ch/gov/en/start/documentation/media-releases/media-releases-federal-council.msg-id-84035.html

The White House. (2022, March 9). *Executive Order on Ensuring Responsible Development of Digital Assets.* https://www.whitehouse.gov/briefing-room/presidential-actions/2022/03/09/executive-order-on-ensuring-responsible-development-of-digital-assets/

Tokengate. (n.d.). *Allow us to make you look like a token genius.* Retrieved March 23, 2022, from https://www.tokengate.io/invest

Tokeny. (2020, December 15). *Digibrixx Democratizes Real Estate via Tokenization.* https://tokeny.com/digibrixx-democratizes-real-estate-via-tokenization/

Upadhyay, A., Mukhuty, S., Kumar, V., & Kazancoglu, Y. (2021). Blockchain technology and the circular economy: Implications for sustainability and social responsibility. *Journal of Cleaner Production, 293*, 126130. https://doi.org/10.1016/j.jclepro.2021.126130

Upvest. (2020, December). *Partnership with Upvest.* https://crowdlitoken.com/news/partnership-with-upvest/?lang=en

Veuger, J. (2017). Attention to disruption and blockchain creates a viable real estate economy. *Journal of US-China Public Administration, 14*(5), 263–285. https://doi.org/10.17265/1548-6591/2017.05.003

Wouda, H., & Opdenakker, R. (2019). Blockchain technology in commercial real estate transactions. *Journal of Property Investment & Finance, 37*(6), 570–579. https://doi.org/10.1108/JPIF-06-2019-0085

Wüst, K., & Gervais, A. (2018). Do you need a Blockchain? [Conference session]. 2018 Crypto Valley Conference on Blockchain Technology (CVCBT), Zug, Switzerland. https://doi.org/10.1109/CVCBT.2018.00011

Yaga, D., Mell, P., Roby, N., & Scarfone, K. (2018). *Blockchain technology overview.* National Institute of Standards and Technology, US Department of Commerce. https://doi.org/10.48550/arXiv.1906.11078

Yin, R. (2014). *Case study research design and methods* (5th ed.).

Yli-Huumo, J., Ko, D., Choi, S., Park, S., & Smolander, K. (2016). Where is current research on blockchain technology?-a systematic review. *PLoS One, 11*(10). https://doi.org/10.1371/journal.pone.0163477

Zheng, Z., Xie, S., Dai, H., Chen, X., & Wang, H. (2017). An overview of blockchain technology: Architecture, consensus, and future trends [Conference session]. 2017 IEEE international congress on big data (BigData congress), Honolulu, USA. https://doi.org/10.1109/BigDataCongress.2017.85.

Zheng, Z., Xie, S., Dai, H., Chen, X., & Wang, H. (2018). Blockchain challenges and opportunities: A survey. *International Journal of Web and Grid Services, 14*(4), 353–371. https://doi.org/10.1504/IJWGS.2018.095647

Zheng, Z., Xie, S., Dai, H.-N., Chen, W., Chen, X., Weng, J., & Imran, M. (2020). An overview on smart contracts: Challenges, advances and platforms. *Future Generation Computer Systems, 105*, 475–491. https://doi.org/10.1016/j.future.2019.12.019

Zhou, Q., Huang, H., Zheng, Z., & Bian, J. (2020). Solutions to scalability of blockchain: A survey. *IEEE Access, 8*, 16440–16455. https://doi.org/10.1109/ACCESS.2020.2967218

GPSR Compliance
The European Union's (EU) General Product Safety Regulation (GPSR) is a set of rules that requires consumer products to be safe and our obligations to ensure this.

If you have any concerns about our products, you can contact us on

ProductSafety@springernature.com

In case Publisher is established outside the EU, the EU authorized representative is:

Springer Nature Customer Service Center GmbH
Europaplatz 3
69115 Heidelberg, Germany

www.ingramcontent.com/pod-product-compliance
Ingram Content Group UK Ltd.
Pitfield, Milton Keynes, MK11 3LW, UK
UKHW020704041026
15590UKWH00001B/460
* 9 7 8 3 0 3 1 5 5 8 0 9 2 *